P9-BYY-813

YOU AND THE NEW MORALITY

YOU &

THE NEW MORALITY

-74 Cases

James A. Pike

HARPER & ROW, PUBLISHERS

NEW YORK, EVANSTON, AND LONDON

YOU & THE NEW MORALITY. *Copyright © 1967 by James A. Pike. Printed in the United States of America. All rights reserved. No part of this book may be used or reproduced in any manner whatsoever without written permission except in the case of brief quotations embodied in critical articles and reviews. For information address Harper & Row, Publishers, Incorporated, 49 East 33rd Street, New York, N.Y. 10016.*

FIRST EDITION

LIBRARY OF CONGRESS CATALOG CARD NUMBER: 67-14935

TO MY SON

Chris

MANY THANKS

Since this is a casebook, I owe most to my many counselees over the years, through whom I have grown in experience and insight. I have been enlightened, too, by others espousing situation ethics, including a number whom I count as friends: Prof. Joseph Fletcher of the Episcopal Theological School (*Situation Ethics* [Philadelphia: Westminster Press, 1966]), Bishop John A. T. Robinson (*Honest to God* and *A New Reformation?* [Westminster Press, 1963, 1965]), Canon Douglas Rhymes of Southwark Cathedral (*No New Morality* [New York: J. B. Lippincott, 1965]), and the Cambridge theologians who took me into their fellowship when I was on sabbatical in England last year (including essayists in *Soundings* [Cambridge University Press, 1962] and *Objections to Christian Belief* [London: Constable & Co., 1963]).

Near to the scene and the production of this effort thanks are due to the staff of New Focus agency, who implement my "public" life (speaking, writing, etc.), especially Mrs. Maren Bergrud, who contributed much to both thought and form. And also to my colleagues at the Center for the Study of Democratic Institutions, for the civilization of dialogue and stimulus to a critical view toward one's own notions.

All biblical quotations, except when otherwise noted, are from the Revised Standard Version.

THE METHOD

In the widespread and serious debate today between the proponents of systems of ethics—non-normative existentialism ("I do what I do"), situation-weighing ("It depends"), and application of the conventional code ("I always/I never"), there is one great lack. Most of the contenders deal in abstractions—even the existentialists, who purportedly eschew abstractions. Of course, a few examples are given, generally of the tea-and-sympathy type or cloak-and-dagger type, but one does not get the feeling that the analysis or conclusions drawn have really emerged from common, real-life encounters.

With the hope of making some contribution to what is one of the most important dialogues of our time, the author will revert to the approach customary in his first professional discipline, the Case Method used in law study and legal analysis. Granted, no patterns can be formulated without a measure of deduction, or at least inference. But it is to be presumed that any conclusions drawn will be sounder if they are grounded in the inductive process.

So about half of what follows consists of cases. Some of these, too, are unrealistic—as is appropriate to the use of the *reductio ad absurdum* approach to certain ethical theories. But most (with appropriate alterations in the interests of anonymity, clarity, and brevity) represent real situations. The text, apart from the cases, does not constitute a manual of moral theology. It will serve, as in some law books, as commentary, meant to focus piecemeal various issues that arise out of a group of related cases. If the relatively brief summary at the end has any value, it will be because of the author's and the readers' analysis of various categories of cases along the way. It is further assumed—and hoped—that the cases presented here suggest to the minds of the readers other illustrations which are as alive, or more alive, to them because of their own personal or vicarious experience.

It would be a violation of the method to spell out more at this point. Let's get down to cases.

✠ JAMES A. PIKE

Center for the Study of Democratic Institutions
Santa Barbara, California
Thanksgiving Day, 1966

CONTENTS

chapter 1

LET'S START WITH SEX

case 1. "We're all happier now"

John, a married man, and Mary, a single career woman, have been seeing each other regularly for a couple of years and have been expressing their love for each other in intimate relationship for about eighteen months. They have felt that this is "all right," John for an external reason and Mary for an internal one. For years John's wife, Joan, has been an alcoholic, and during the last four or five years her chronic alcoholism has been so compulsive and severe that all measures have failed and she has increasingly become a "vegetable," uninterested in anything, including her husband—either in general sharing or in sexual relations. A psychiatrist has found permanent brain damage, but her schizophrenic symptoms have not signaled sufficient danger to herself or anyone else to warrant institutionalizing her—especially in the light of her strong opposition to any such solution.

Mary, on the other hand, has found her practice of the law sufficiently engrossing for a good many years for her to have known that she did not want to get married, and thus she has not felt that her abiding relationship with John is blocking her from what with others would be the fulfillment of hope for marriage. John and Mary do not feel that Joan is being robbed of anything. In fact, since he has been intimate with Mary, he has been noticeably more patient with Joan's unresponsiveness and more attentive to her needs—real or supposed. Instances of tension between John and Mary are infrequent and short-lived.

case 2. "We're not hurting anyone"

Bill and Alice are happily married in a kind of taken-for-granted way. He began to be thrown together a good deal with Dorothy, a married girl at the office, whose marriage was solvent enough but who actually shared more of Bill's interests than those of her husband Jack. One night when she planned to stay over in the city because she had been asked to work quite late with Bill on a rush project, they concluded their work with a few nightcaps. Bill decided to stay in town also.

From that night on they renewed their intimate relations as often as opportunity was afforded. Each assured the other that there was no intention of breaking up either marriage; in fact, each affirmed—and apparently meant it—love of the spouse. But both agreed that their relationship was very meaningful and added to the fullness and joy of life. Yet there was no question that, while sexual relations continued unabated at home, intercourse was more exciting and more eagerly anticipated in the case of their own liaison.

case 3. One-night stand

Murray and Mildred, both single, got acquainted during a long weekend in a town some distance from their own homes, where they had gone as members of a wedding party. They rather naturally "took to" each other, though neither very seriously. On returning to their hotel the last night they decided that it would be more pleasant to sleep in one room than in two. The next morning they took their leave and returned home, each expressing the hope that their paths would cross again.

case 4. Services rendered

Joe, a married man, was sent by his firm to Tokyo for a month. Having time on his hands evenings, several times he engaged in relations with prostitutes, treating them kindly and expressing his appreciation with a tip each time.

We start with examples all from the field of sex behavior for three reasons:

1. This is what is expected. Most people who have heard the phrase "the new morality" automatically associate it with the topic of sex. And understandably enough: our culture, still affected by its conditioning through both Puritan and pietistic influences, has long tended to associate the noun "morality" in the phrase with sex. For example, if we hear that a clergyman has been unfrocked for immorality we just assume that he was caught in some fort of hetero- or homosexual activity. Our imaginations would be unlikely to conjure up an image of his stealing from the alms basin or breaking the seal of Confession or remaining silent in the face of grave social evil, such as racial discrimination —though, on reflection, many would readily agree that these forms of conduct are also immoral.

2. It is in connection with sex that there is the greatest degree of nervousness about the adjective "new." Since the old morality has been conceived as the bastion of conven-

tional sexual behavior, it is assumed that the adjective connotes undifferentiated endorsement of everything up to free love. The very fact of the presentation of four quite different illustrations with various complexities to be weighed should suggest right at the beginning that this work will not turn out to be a piece of propaganda for an amoral stance.

3. If illustrations from the field of sex were delayed until farther along in the volume, all through the pages up to that point there would lurk in some readers' minds either the suspicion that the subject was being dodged through an exaggerated sense of propriety, or the fear that their agreement with anything but absolutist principles in connection with cases in other fields might logically lead them, unaware, to liberal conclusions in cases about sex. So at least all is out in the open from the beginning.

It would be premature, however, to seek to analyze these four illustrations right now. Two other tasks have priority.

First, we should consider bases for deciding what scheme of ethics is the most acceptable one, what frame of reference should consistently be used in making particular ethical decisions. In the end there are only three such schemes: Code ethics, founded on immutable laws derived from an infallible source or sources; antinomianism (literally, against-law-ism); and existential ethics, grounded in a claim upon the individual to make decisions responsibly but with the understanding that each decision must be made in a context of the given situation, and that no a priori answer book is possible.

Second, if the last of these schemes should appear to be the most convincing (or at least worthy of consideration), then we should focus on factors that should be taken into account in the process of deciding among schemes of ethics. Thus equipped, with more prospect of sound answers to our questions, we can return to cases like the four with which we have opened.

But we begin with the first task, and will seek to test the soundness of the three major schools of ethics through the case method.

The view most generally accepted, at least on the conscious level, is that of Code ethics. Some people support the Code simply because that is what they have been taught. Many people, however, support their affirmation of it on a basis of some selected authority or combination of authorities. The principal bases are these: the Ten Commandments, other Biblical injunctions, the teaching of the Church, and natural law. We will proceed in this order.

chapter 2

THE TEN COMMANDMENTS?

case 5. Graven images I

The new church of St. Peter's-by-the-Sea, while quite economical and utilitarian, is so "contemporary" that it doesn't strike its members as looking like a church. A gifted woman sculptor, a member of the congregation, carved out of redwood an imaginative figure of the Patron holding an outsize key. Placed up high against the blank surface on the left of the entry, it has changed the whole character of the building. Whether out of dislike for the particular sculpture or for the artist, or out of genuine Biblical conviction, the Chairman of the Fabric Committee has raised a question about the Commandment "Thou shalt not make unto thyself any graven images." The vicar's opinion is asked.

case 6. Graven images II

In the late Middle Ages there was widespread religious inspiration and also superstition in connection with the shrine of St. Thomas à Becket at Canterbury Cathedral.

King Henry VIII was aware of this; but he was even more sensitive to the fact that pilgrimages to the shrine and acts of devotion there had long been a way of manifesting opposition to the policies of the crown. As chief of state and head of the Church he ordered the destruction of the shrine, an act presumably within his dual authority. Is ethical consideration of any other pros and cons foreclosed by the literal application of the Second Commandment?

case 7. G-d for God?

Contrary to popular impression, the Third Commandment, "Thou shalt not take the name of the Lord, thy God, in vain," had nothing originally to do with cursing. Those who passed on to us this Commandment believed that God had revealed to Moses His true Name, the tetragrammaton *YHWH*, and that this word was too holy to be uttered. Accordingly, a designation all men recognized as being humanly derived, *Elohim* (literally, gods), was used to communicate the concept. Even today, an Orthodox Jew using the English language will write "G-d," not "God." Should the rest of us adopt this precaution?

case 8. Church on Saturday?

Again, contrary to a commonly accepted view which causes conservative Church groups to refer to "Sabbath schools" and "Sabbath observance," the Christian Sunday, as the principal day for worship, has no connection whatsoever—Biblically, historically, or ideologically—with the Jewish Sabbath. Roman Catholic churches with a resident priest and some Episcopal churches provide an opportunity for worship on the Sabbath, but simply because there are services every day. But the attendance is quite minimal and is not especially urged. Churches of other denominations will more than likely be found locked on the Sabbath. There are two exceptions: the Seventh Day Adventists and the Seventh Day Baptists. Should the other denominations not concede that they are right and change their habits of worship?

case 9. Honor a dishonorable father?

Colonel Brown has been court-martialed on a charge which, if proven, will bring him at the least a dishonorable discharge. His son, a second lieutenant, is one of the two witnesses available to provide evidence in support of the charge. If he tells the truth, far from honoring his father, he will contribute to the denigration of his father's entire military career. Shall he lie under oath to obey the Fifth Commandment, "Honor thy father . . . ," or shall he tell the truth in obedience to the Ninth Commandment, "Thou shalt not bear false witness"?

case 10. Killing for not killing

Recently a Jehovah's Witness, drafted into the Greek army, was sentenced to death for twice refusing to bear arms because of his religious convictions. Since there is no exemption in that country for conscientious objection, should this young Greek have obeyed the law, or was he right to insist on obeying the Sixth Commandment, "Thou shalt not kill"? Were his Greek Orthodox Christian judges right in disobeying the Commandment in order to have him killed for refusing to disobey the Commandment—or for any other cause? (The sentence was subsequently commuted.)

case 11. Ready to break two

The two Commandments "Thou shalt not commit adultery" and "Thou shalt not kill" are, of course, in the Bible. But also bound in the Bibles of by far the majority of Christians (Roman Catholics, Eastern Orthodox, and Anglicans) is the story of Judith.[1] The heroine goes forth from besieged Jerusalem prepared to go to bed with the Syrian commander Holofernes so that she might have the opportunity of stabbing him to death and thus freeing her nation. (The fact that his intemperance after he proffered refreshments happily relieved her of the necessity of committing adultery in order to get close enough to kill him does not change the character of her prior moral decision.) When his comrades in arms found him mysteriously dead early the next morning, they fled in superstitious fear; and the city was free again. She is a heroine of Israel, and ever since, Jewish and Christian parents have honored her by naming daughters after her. But should she have been willing to break two of the Commandments?

case 12. The stolen love letter

Patricia Smith, long aware of her husband's pattern of infidelity, had been unsuccessful—through either persuasion or threat—in changing the situation, and had also been unsuccessful, after she had given up hope for the marriage, in securing his consent to a divorce. The only ground at the time in New York was adultery. Certain as she was of his infidelities, she lacked legal evidence. One day, in emptying the pockets of one of her husband's suits before

[1] The Articles of Religion (of the Anglican Churches) includes the Book of Judith among the "books (as Hierome saith)" which the Church does "not apply . . . to establish any doctrine," but reads "for example of life and instruction of manners" (Article VI).

sending it to the cleaners, she ran across an opened letter whose contents were explicit to the point of vulgarity and supplied evidence aplenty. Should she simply have placed it on his bedside table, following the Commandment "Thou shalt not steal"; or should she have taken it to her lawyer?

case 13. Lying—but patriotically

Herbert Worthy, a C.I.A. agent, has been arrested in mainland China on charges of espionage. The evidence against him is strong enough for him to see no point in not telling the truth under oath on the witness stand, so far as any hope goes of avoiding the death sentence. But to tell the truth would endanger his nation and other agents currently working in China. He has figured out a way to cover, appearing to be candid—thus avoiding the possibility of torture and at the same time revealing nothing damaging. On this basis may he ignore the clear Commandment "Thou shalt not bear false witness"?[2]

case 14. The haves and have-nots

Not long ago a large number of grape-pickers in and around Delano, California, engaged in strikes and demonstrations because they desired to have a larger share of the profits of the grape and winery industry, coveting some of what had been going to the growers and vintners. Similarly, "have-nots," for example in Latin American countries, have sought by political or revolutionary means to secure

[2] It is true that the Commandment ends with the words, "against thy neighbor." Apart from the fact that the Commandment has been generally applied to prohibit all lying, the New Testament gives the word "neighbor" universal application, including enemies.

the breakup of large estates owned by the landed classes. Should they have restrained their actions on the basis of the Commandment "Thou shalt not covet . . . anything that is thy neighbor's"?

On the face of things, examples like these would seem to discredit the claim that the Ten Commandments represent the absolute moral law. Nevertheless those who desire to maintain the absoluteness of the Commandments have been known to answer such illustrations in two ways:

1. They will point out that they are quite aware that the Commandments are often disobeyed. (In fact, they rather seem to expect this if, tutored by St. Paul, St. Augustine, and Calvin, they couple rigidity about the Commandments with the doctrine of the total depravity of man.) But they will insist, quite rightly, that failure to observe a Commandment does not nullify the Commandment. Some of these protagonists, of a kindlier sort, might even grant that in such "hardship" cases there may be strong pressures exerted on the unlucky decision-makers and they might even have some sympathy for those in such a plight. Such a response is relatively trivial—and at best sentimental—compared with the real issue: the serious claim which in each case runs up against the given Commandment.

2. Many absolutists about the Commandments would readily enough grant that in one or another of the cases the one who decides is probably right in breaking the Commandment, but they would regard this as an exception to what is still an absolute rule. But for one who thinks of ethics in terms of absolutes, that is, of principles built-in in the universe or representing the revealed will of God, there is no room for the category of "exception." The greatest expositor of absolutes among Christian theologians, St.

Thomas Aquinas, also took pains to point out (following Aristotle) that a *negative particular destroys an affirmative universal;* that is, something "universal" cannot sometimes not be universal. The absolutist is not saved from this logic by a supposition that such "particulars" occur very rarely indeed. To begin with, such a supposition already is in the arena of fact and not of theory, and hence there is nothing valid which the absolutist could say on the score of the rarity or infrequency of these troublesome exceptions (unless he could back up his assumptions with a professionally sponsored anthropological and sociological study—or at least a Gallup Poll). But even if one could estimate the degree of frequency of the exceptions on any acceptable empirical basis, when one case is conceded there is no longer a viable "universal" to provide the automatic answers that the absolutist finds so desirable.

In short, whatever value we may find we can attribute to the Ten Commandments, it is clear that they do not supply a basis for Code ethics.

There are those who seek to avoid the difficulty of the literal application of the Commandments in any or all cases by taking this line: We should recognize that the Ten Commandments were spoken to a different culture a long time ago; therefore to have them speak to us, we must discern the spirit of each Commandment—the abiding principle that lies behind it—and reapply each to our own time.

For example, the real concern of the Second Commandment, against graven images, was not the manufacture of them as such, but the worshiping of them. Their construction was forbidden to make completely sure that there would be no images to worship. But since, the argument would run, there is no danger that anyone would worship an image, we need not regard the literal prohibition of the Commandment as a barrier to edifying iconography.

Or, to take another example, the purpose of the prohibition against voicing God's name was to protect against irreverence; today people are not irreverent in speaking the name of God, except when they are cursing—so that act is what the Commandment should be regarded as forbidding.

Then again, the Fourth Commandment was meant to set aside a day each week for the corporate worship of God; custom early changed this from Saturday to Sunday for Christians—so for us the injunction of the Commandment is applicable to Sundays.

But these "common sense" reshapings of the Commandments are not unaccompanied by further difficulties. In particular as to the Second Commandment, Christians are not agreed—and for good reason—that there is no danger that statues and other images will become the focus of worship. The Eastern Orthodox Churches to this day do not permit three-dimensional representations; some Protestant denominations do not allow any representations. And in some cultures where the predominant denomination does make widespread use of sculpture and relics, it would appear that in fact there is considerable superstition—sometimes carried over from the area's pre-Christian cults; at least some observers who are more enlightened members of the same Church have so indicated.

To consider the modern application of the Third Commandment, views range from that of the modern-day Orthodox Jew, who is convinced that the nonutterance of the name of God is an important factor in reverent response to Him, to that of the liberal Christian, who, quite apart from aesthetic judgment about swearing, would not regard these expletives as really irreverent since the one using them is not in fact talking—or even thinking—about God at all.

Regarding the Fourth Commandment, not only do not all Christians agree that the switch from Saturday to Sunday is licit, but Christians disagree as to the character of the observance. Many have sought to retain, but simply on a different day, the restriction of normal activities and pleasures; others see Sunday, except for a brief period spent in church, as another day off—like the modern Saturday. And some Churches do not teach that failing to go to church is a sin; even in the Roman Catholic Church today some are urging that it not longer be so regarded.

But, quite apart from such specific difficulties, there is an over-all one. For the task of going behind the dictates to the spirit or principle and then reapplying the Commandments with new definitions for today, *some norm outside the Commandments themselves* is being used in different Church traditions. The process itself demonstrates that the Commandments as such are not absolute.

What is the super-Commandment norm? It is one of the following: (a) we are to take the New Testament into account in interpreting the Old; (b) the Church has the authority to interpret the Commandments (which is to say that it is really the Church's teaching which is absolute); (c) the natural law lying behind the words of the Commandment is what is final; or (d) whatever we now do is what we ought to do; but, as we have seen, "I do what I do" is antinomianism.

Each of these possible norms will be given separate treatment in the chapters that follow. Since we have been considering the Old Testament Commandments, we will turn first to the New Testament as a norm. It will simplify things to point out right away that nothing reported as from Jesus contradicts, qualifies, or modifies the Ten Commandments. Texts relating to the Commandments accept them at face value—that is, literally—and then sometimes give them more stringent applications. A good example is "You have heard that it was said, 'You shall not commit adultery.' But I say to you that every one who looks at a woman lustfully has already committed adultery with her in his heart" (Matt. 5:27–28). But in the Gospels we find directives and prohibitions additional to those given in the Ten Commandments. Hence we should give consideration to the absolute character of these injunctions.

chapter 3

OTHER BIBLICAL INJUNCTIONS

case 15. Turn the other cheek?

Johnny, 10, had just come home with a black eye. His father asked him where he got it. Johnny said that he'd been hit by a lad, 12, who had been bullying Johnny and others in the neighborhood for some time. "Then what did you do?" his father asked. "I knocked him down." His father smiled and nodded his head. His mother said, "Oh, you shouldn't have done that!" and quoted the text about turning the other cheek (Matt. 5:39b). "You mean that he should have asked that bully to blacken his other eye?" her husband asked incredulously. "Well," his wife answered, "if we're going to live by the Bible . . ." On this score, of course, she was quite right. But Johnny's father had for some time been concerned about the inferiority feelings which the older lad's consistent behavior had been engendering in his son and valued the note of confidence he heard in Johnny's voice when he told of how he had responded. Further, he was glad a group of the neighborhood kids were around to see it. He had reason to believe that the older boy's bullying days were over. Who is right?

case 16. Take California too!

After the Japanese attack on Pearl Harbor the United States immediately declared war. Should we have turned the other cheek? After Japan successfully invaded and took the Philippine Islands, following the injunction in the Sermon on the Mount, "From him who takes away your cloak, do not withhold your coat as well" (Luke 6:29), should we have offered them California? Should we, from December 7, 1941, right through, simply have followed the command, "Do not resist one who is evil" (Matt. 5:39a)?

case 17. Empty out your wallet?

In his parish church on Sunday night Mr. Trevor Eastburn, an Episcopal lay reader, read the Second Lesson, and it was the portion of the Sermon on the Mount including the cloak/coat command just quoted. When the service was over he had not walked three blocks from the sacristy, where he had unvested, when he was held up by a thug who took about fifty dollars in bills from his wallet. Mr. Eastburn noticed that the thief had not discovered the fifty-dollar bill which he had kept hidden behind his credit cards. Recalling the lesson he had just read, the thought crossed his mind, Should I offer him this bill too? Should he have acted out the thought?

case 18. Anonymity/publicity?

In responding generously to a campaign for funds for a church home for unmarried mothers, Mr. Pendleton Harris desired to keep the gift anonymous for fear that knowledge of this gift might make him a sitting duck for other solicitations. But he thought of the text which had been used as the

Offertory Sentence the Sunday before, "Let your light so shine before men, that they may see your good works and give glory to your Father who is in heaven" (Matt. 5:16). Should he let his name be listed?

case 19. Publicity/anonymity?

In responding generously to the same campaign, Mr. Wilfred Bartlett wanted to give his name and secure a receipt for substantiation of his contemplated income tax deduction. But he recalled from a lesson read at the same service the words, "But when you give alms, do not let your left hand know what your right hand is doing, so that your alms may be in secret; and your Father [rather than the Bureau of Internal Revenue] who sees in secret will reward you" (Matt 6:3–4). Should he give his gift anonymously?

case 20. Swearing on the Bible

A witness in court, as a matter of course, was sworn in. After he had uttered the words, his eye dropped to the volume which had been placed under his hands. Noting that it was the Holy Bible, there flashed through his mind the words, "You have heard that it was said to the men of old, You shall not swear falsely. . . . But I say to you, Do not swear at all . . . Let what you say be simply 'Yes' or 'No'; anything more than this comes from evil" (Matt. 5:33, 37).[1] Should he have the oath stricken from the record and substitute instead the affirmation allowed as an

[1] Cf. Article XXXIX of the (Anglican) Articles of Religion: "A man may swear when the Magistrate requireth . . . so it be done . . . in justice, judgment and truth."

alternate in most jurisdictions? Or should he go on with his testimony?

case 21. "Where moth and rust doth corrupt"

A rubric on page 320 of the Book of Common Prayer reads, "The minister is ordered, from time to time, to advise the People, whilst they are in health, to make Wills arranging for the disposal of their temporal goods, and, when of ability, to leave Bequests for religious and charitable uses." Would an appropriate answer to this not too subtle request for provision of capital for the Church be the prohibition "Do not lay up for yourselves treasures on earth . . ." (Matt. 6:19)? Similarly, is the whole banking business basically unethical?

case 22. Eunuch for the Kingdom's sake?

Eric, a young man of 25, is a Lutheran. He has always taken seriously his religion and its moral teachings. He is in love with a young lady whom he has known for some time, and he has every reason to believe that their marriage would be a happy one. At the same time, he is quite aware that at no time before or after becoming acquainted with her, has control over sexual desires been a problem with him; and, as a regular Bible reader he has been struck by the applicability of two passages. The first are the words attributed to Jesus, ". . . there are eunuchs who have been so from birth, and there are eunuchs who have been made eunuchs by men, and there are eunuchs who have made themselves eunuchs for the sake of the Kingdom of heaven. He who is able to receive this, let him receive it" (Matt. 19:12). Second, the words of Paul: "It is well for a man not to touch a woman. . . . To the unmarried and the widows I say that it is well for them to remain single as I do. But if they cannot exercise self-control, they should marry" (1 Cor 7:1, 8–9). He knows that, consistent with these texts, the Roman Catholic Church (with less emphasis since the period of the recent Vatican Council, to be sure) has exalted celibacy as a higher ethic than marriage. And, while the flat rejection of this very notion was one of the fundamentals of the Reformation which brought his Church into being, another fundamental was the infallibility of the Scriptures as against any traditions of any Church.[2] Eric seems to fit precisely into the category of those called to celibacy by the scriptural words quoted. Further, the particular Lutheran body in which he was raised always stressed the literal interpretation of the Bible, and the words quoted from Jesus literally refer to castration, and the words were so understood by holy ones living nearer the time. Should he seek a cooperative surgeon? Should he "mythologize" a bit and simply decide for the single state?

[2] "A problem which was shirked by the Second Vatican Council, but will have to be faced by Catholic scholarship, is whether it still serves a purpose to retain the traditional view of the Scriptures as divinely inspired. The wide divergence of views held on the contents of the Bible, the degree of demythologization imposed even by non-radical scholarship, the carefree attitude of the ancient authors towards their 'historical' sources and the corrections we are forced to make even in the religious views of the books of the Old Testament, and other reasons, make it futile and impossible to equate the truth of the Bible with the meaning intended by its authors. The fact also that a belief in inspiration is not restricted to the Hebrews, but in some form was held by the ancients of many lands—e.g., the Hindus and Persians, Greeks and Romans—makes it all but certain that we are faced with the common reaction of more primitive people toward phenomena they could not explain naturally.—A change in perspective, as has occurred in the view on the origin of

Numerous other cases could be developed which would illustrate the problem of applying various New Testament texts to real problems of life. But the recitation would not add to the point which should already be quite apparent from our assortment of illustrations, namely, that we do not find a basis for an absolute Code ethic in the New Testament. And if cases were added involving texts that could receive a clearly positive application, this would not solve the problem because the very process of endorsing some texts and of dismissing or qualifying others *presupposes an outside norm of judgment.* If such a norm is found to be sound, then is not it, rather than the New Testament, the absolute?

There are three possible answers:

1. As we have seen in the case of the Ten Commandments, it is proposed that we go behind the literal text and discern the spirit of it or the principle which it embodies and reapply it in a contemporary way. Here the answer is the same as it was for the Ten Commandments. Apart from differences, in each instance, among Christians on whether to be literal or to demythologize about what the implicit principle really is and how it is to be applied if discovered, to the degree that such a process is successful there is involved the application of some other system of absolutes

---

man, may be expected in our beliefs in regard to the origin of Scriptures. Former positions on the contents of the Bible and the meaning of inspiration have already been so largely modified or abandoned by a number of Catholic scholars that the value of the Bible for religion does not seem to require belief in inspiration. On balance, belief in divine inspiration has probably been for some centuries—and still is—the occasion of more harm than good to the cause of religion." Most Reverend Francis Simons, (Roman Catholic) Bishop of Indore, India, in "The Catholic Church and the New Morality," *Cross Currents,* vol., XVI, no. 4, Fall, 1966.

external to the New Testament Commandments themselves.

2. Some moral theologians have sought a way out through interpreting the words of Jesus in the light of the fact that He and the Evangelists, and Paul as well, expected the imminent end of the existing order of things through the coming of the Son of Man and His angels to establish a new earthly kingdom. The various black-and-white absolutes in the New Testament are seen as an "interim ethic."[3] For example, for one expecting all the present conditions of personal life and social institutions soon to end suddenly with the blowing of a trumpet, it would seem quite sensible for a Paul to say, in effect, "If you're married, stay that way; if you're not married, don't get married—unless you just have to." And similarly, under these circumstances, why be concerned about a new suit of clothes or adding to the larder? Or why care what anybody takes away from you; give it to him—and more. None of these things will be needed in the Kingdom, which is just around the corner.

But it would seem that the fact of this eschatological distortion would lead to an obvious conclusion: "the new morality" spoken in the shadow of it is irrelevant in a world with a different view of history. Nineteen hundred years have gone by and such divine intervention has not occurred, and there is no particular reason to assume that it is going to.[4] So of what use has been—or will be—this interim ethic?

[3] See Paul Ramsey, *Basic Christian Ethics* (New York: Charles Scribner's Sons, 1950), p. 34; cf. the present author's *What Is This Treasure?* (New York: Harper & Row, 1966), p. 54.

[4] The Roman Catholic theologian Professor Leslie Dewart has recently written: ". . . once it no longer has 'God's omnipotence' to fall back on, our Christian conscience may be awakened to feel its adult responsibilities for taking the full initiative in 'restoring all things in Christ' and for exercising its creative ingenuity in order

But this is not the conclusion drawn by the moral theologians of the eschatological school. Rather, they say: the very fact that the imminent end was expected gives to these ethical insights an absoluteness and purity which provides for us the white by which we can judge varying shades of gray in making decisions within a context which assumes that history, personal and societal, simply goes on.

Let's check this out against some of the Cases already given.

CASE 15. *Turn the other cheek?* If one should decide that, all things considered, the bullied ten-year-old did right to strike back (given the unendorsable bullying as a fact), then his conduct was not a "gray" as compared with the "white" of presenting his other eye to be blackened.

CASE 16. *Take California too!* Whatever evils can be discerned, on hindsight, in the attitudes and actions of Japan and the United States which would seem to have contributed to the attack on Pearl Harbor, the attack having been made, if the sounder decision was national self-defense, then allowing more of our territory to be dominated without resistance is not some *ideal* with which the exigencies of historical life have compelled us to compromise. Here, to follow the Biblical texts cited could be evil.

CASE 17. *Empty out your wallet?* Not to resist the thief at gun point would seem to be the sounder decision; but, when no risk to life compels it, to dig up for him an additional fifty dollars does not represent a particularly good

---

to determine how this should be done. For we will then no longer expect miracles to happen (least of all the miracle of the glorious appearance of the Christ upon a cloud), and we will instead believe that, unless we make it be, the Kingdom of God shall never come." *The Future of Belief* (London: Herder & Herder, 1966), pp. 193–94.

application of the stewardship of means. To keep the analogy of colors, the unnecessary overpayment would not be white, but rather black or at least a dark shade of gray.

And a quick second glance at the other Cases would suggest that it would work out about the same way. So, as sound exegetically as the eschatological reading of New Testament ethical declarations is, the attempt to argue from this premise to the absolute character of the declarations obviously overshoots the mark.

3. Other moral theologians of the Catholic tradition, mainly Roman, Anglican, or Orthodox, press quite a different approach. They maintain that as the Church, the Old and the New Israel, is the source of Holy Scripture and its guardian, so also it is its proper interpreter. Hence the unchanging "teaching of the Church" provides us with an absolute Code. It is now appropriate, through some selected cases, to examine this claim.

chapter 4

THE TEACHING OF THE CHURCH?

case 23. Sin in 1920/duty in 1958

Cynthia Wickfield is one of eight children born of poor parents in England. Their family barely maintained a subsistence level, through charity from their parish church and generous acquaintances. They had not practiced birth control because of the Anglican teaching which received formal expression in the Lambeth Conference of 1920, at which the archbishops and bishops of the Anglican Communion throughout the world solemnly declared any form of contraception to be sinful. Her husband has an extremely modest income, and having had four children in a row she has been unable to leave them to go to work to augment the family income.

Once when Cynthia's parish priest called she expressed the conviction that she and her husband shared, namely, that they should not have more children, and mentioned, regretfully, the teaching of the Church as she had learned it from her parents. "But didn't you know," the rector responded cheerfully, "that the Lambeth Conference of 1958 not only reversed that, but declared that family planning is a moral duty?" She didn't know. Part of her was glad to hear it; but another part of her was puzzled. Perhaps she was being naïve; but she wondered how something that would have been a sin for her parents had now become a duty for her—even though the duty matched her and her husband's preference.

case 24. Ecclesiastical Renos?

Donald and Ronald, twin brothers, had each had an unfortunate marriage. Both marriages seemed to have a promising start. Five years later Donald's wife began to drink more and more heavily. Over the years her alcoholism, with accompanying neglect and bitter hostility, reached a point which made living together impossible. After the first three years the wife of Ronald entered into a pattern of repeated infidelities, on which neither persuasion nor threats had any effect. Donald endured his situation patiently for some years and then procured a divorce. A few months later he fell in love with one of his associates at the office, a young widow. An Episcopalian, he took up the matter of his hopes for marriage with the Reverend Mr. Blanton, who helped Donald prepare an application to the Bishop of Central Connecticut for a judgment on his right to remarry under the canon law of the Church. The request was granted on the ground of the "spiritual death" of the marriage, and Mr. Blanton married the couple a year ago in the parish church.

Donald's brother, Ronald, also an active Episcopalian, had obtained a divorce two years before and a year later met a lovely single woman at a parish supper. As the friendship grew in depth, he discussed the matter with

Father Worthington, his rector. He could perceive no defect at the time of the first marriage which was listed in the canon law as an impediment to matrimony. Accordingly, he expressed doubt that the diocesan, the Bishop of Northern Iowa, would be able to rule favorably. Indeed the latter required strict grounds for ecclesiastical annulment, not recognizing the right to remarry after the spiritual death of a union.[1] Nevertheless he forwarded Ronald's papers; but the judgment was negative. To put it mildly, Ronald was offended by the fact that his second marriage would have been regarded as permissible and valid in the eyes of the Church had he happened to have lived nearer his brother, in Central Connecticut.

case 25. If not consecutively, concurrently?

Joseph Mwambi, who lives in the bush country in Malawi, decided that he and his family should be baptized. His family included, beside himself, three wives and eleven children. The newly assigned clergyman at the village mission was perplexed. This was the first time this particular problem had come within his pastoral responsibilities, and he was aware of several differing approaches to the matter which were endorsed in different Churches and areas:

a. Mr. Mwambi could retain one of the ladies as his wife and dismiss the overplus.

b. In addition to the children, the wives could be baptized since they were not polygamists (each having only one husband), and the baptism of the husband could be de-

[1] As to the conflicting views on this subject see "Trinity in Unity: Remarriage after Divorce in the Episcopal Church," Appendix A, in the author's *A Time for Christian Candor* (New York: Harper & Row, 1964), pp. 143–44.

ferred until his death bed.

c. The family could remain intact and all be baptized; but thereafter Mr. Mwambi should have marital relations with only one of the wives.

None of these struck the minister as quite satisfactory. As for keeping one wife and sending the others away, apart from the problem of a norm of selection (perhaps this could be resolved on the principle of seniority, like the "lay off" principle in labor relations), the actual result, in the light of the mores and economics of the culture, would doubtless be penury or prostitution for the two dismissed. Also threatened would be the mothers' relationship to their children. The first solution would place an undue burden on the remaining, and doubtless older, wife in the care and raising of the eleven children.

The second solution seemed artificial to the pastor. Baptizing the wives and not baptizing the husband would seem to overlook the fact that, as far as the polygamist pattern went, they were really all in it together, and what if his death occurred in a lonely or remote place?

The third policy (wives retained, but sex with only one) presented two difficulties to Mr. Mwambi's mind. One was suggested by the petition in the Lord's Prayer, "Lead us not into temptation": suppose he and the privileged wife had a serious quarrel one night? Another possibility occurred to the minister, not from a Christian, but from a Jewish, source. He had heard that when the Yemenite Jewish refugees arrived in Israel with several wives, the family was received *as is*—but with the understanding that there could be no replacements. What should he do? Or, if he was a minister of a Church in which such matters are governed by a higher authority, what should the Church's policy be?

case 26. Slavery right; discrimination wrong?

Before a national Church convention is a resolution declaring any form of discrimination on a basis of race to be sinful. In debate, an opponent of the resolution makes this point: "From the time of St. Paul's Epistle to Philemon [recognizing, accepting, and in no wise condemning slavery], until the last century or so [the Episcopal Church, unlike other denominations, did not even condemn it in its General Convention in 1863], men were not adjudged guilty of sin for holding slaves. How can the Church now condemn as sin a much milder bother to people, discrimination in housing or eating places? I have been taught that the Church's moral law is an unchanging one." Can the next speaker, who intends to speak in favor of the resolution, preserve the point in his opponent's last sentence and at the same time give a convincing answer to the point in the question he has raised which precedes it?

case 27. High interest/low interest/no interest

Having heard a persuasive sermon on Sunday on the importance of applying Christian ethics in business, Mr. Alfred Boggs is confronted Monday with a decision on whether to recommend to the board of his bank a 1½ per cent increase in interest rates. There are several practical pros and cons. For the very reason that he is undecided, he becomes interested in what light may be thrown on the problem by moral theology. He has heard of the sin of usury and looks up the word in the dictionary. He finds that the modern meaning is "an exorbitant amount or rate of interest," but that the word had originally meant "a premium for a loan of money or goods" and that the original meaning of "usurer" was "one who lends money, especially at interest." He then looks up the history of the matter and finds that for most of the centuries of the Church's history any taking of interest on loans was declared to be sinful. Before a Sunday night Youth Group at the church, he had recently spoken eloquently of the Church's "unchanging moral law" (of course the subject was sex). He is confused.

To a declaration beginning "The Church teaches . . . ," an obvious answer for these cases (and there could have been many more covering all areas of ethics) is a double-barreled interrogatory: "What Church? Which century?" Long ago a test of what is abiding was stated by St. Vincent of Lerins: *ubique, semper et ab omnibus,* everywhere, always, and by all. A satisfying standard, indeed. But the difficulty is that as we examine the ethical teaching of the Church on various points, both on a comparative basis and on a historical basis, that's not the way it is.

But two answers have been given:

1. Some Churches believe in the infallibility of an ecclesiastical authority, either a council of bishops or a given bishop, and would maintain that the very fact of the issuance of a law by the appropriate authority makes it morally binding under penalty of sin. Thus until recently, in the Roman Catholic Church, the eating of meat on Friday was a mortal sin, except in a few exempted jurisdictions. Now there has been almost universal abandonment of the rule, by action of national Episcopal conferences, acting under papal authority. The same development is true in the case of what had been the sin of receiving Holy Communion without a strict fast from midnight the night before. For those believing in the absolute "now" authority, the fact of change or outright reversal has created no logical problem,

since behavioral demands in such areas have been attributed to "discipline," not to "morals." But in the category of moral conduct, change or reversal does present an unanswerable logical problem. Whereas in the case of "discipline," the sinfulness of the act has been seen as actually created by the authoritative declaration, in the case of other sins, presumably the authority has spoken because the conduct was intrinsically wrong or right.

2. This leads to the second type of answer given. What makes given behavior wrong or right is the natural law or divine revelation expressed in the natural law. We have already considered in earlier chapters how "revealed" Biblical texts fare as bases for moral absolutes. Let us now turn to the claims of natural law as such.

chapter 5

THE NATURAL LAW?

case 28. "A man's home is his castle"

The right of possession of property is a standard principle of the natural law.[1] This principle afforded the principal argument for opponents, in various churches or none, of fair housing legislation in California in the months of campaigning for and against the initiative measure known as Proposition 14, a proposed constitutional amendment affirming absolute property rights.[2]

[1] The support of this principle in Article XXXVIII of the (Anglican) Articles of Religion is interesting: "The Riches and Goods of Christians are not common, as touching the right, title, and possession of the same; as certain Anabaptists do falsely boast. Notwithstanding, every man ought, of such things as he possesseth, liberally to give alms to the poor, according to his ability." Cf. Acts 4:32: ". . . no one saith that any of the things which he possessed was his own, but they had everything in common," in accordance with the teaching and practice of the Essene communities, with which the early Christian congregations would appear to have been in continuity. Cf. Jean Danielou, S.J., *The Dead Sea Scrolls and Primitive Christianity* (New York: New American Library, Mentor-Omega, 1962), p. 121.

[2] The amendment was passed more than 2–1 by the electors of the state, but was subsequently declared unconstitutional by the

How absolute is this principle? After the great London fire in the sixteenth century, regulations on the use of one's property for burning things were adopted by Parliament—limitations analogous to somewhat earlier legislation about garbage. In the last century there has been adopted almost everywhere a variety of zoning restrictions. All along the right of a government to exercise eminent domain has been recognized.[3] Are all these developments intrinsically wrong? And if not, how absolute is the asserted principle of natural law?

case 29. Sin depending upon decade and geography

The denomination of fornication as immoral has been generally supported on the ground of the natural law, with the assumption that this is one of the principles supported by the general consent of mankind. But just a superficial glance at the mores (even ignoring widespread practice) of various times and cultures indicates how nonuniversal this "principle" is. In the early Hebrew culture, for example, passages in the Old Testament give proof of the sanction of unmarried sexual activity on the part of certain persons, e.g., slaves, concubines, and bondwomen[4]—as well as the men who cohabited with them; and until the present day certain South Pacific cultures expected unmarried youth to

State Supreme Court. Later, a popular poll indicated that public opinion against fair housing laws remained 2–1.

[3] The taking of private property for public purposes, in most places presumably with adequate compensation; it is called "expropriation" where adequate compensation is not included in the governmental action.

[4] E.g., Gen. 25:6; Gen. 35:22; Ex. 21; 1 Chron. 3:9; 2 Chron. 12:21; 1 Kings 11:3; Esther 2:14; 2 Sam. 5:13.

engage in sexual activity—and this along with severe penalties for post-marital straying.

Mark, single and 19, has been raised in an unchurchgoing household in which neither the Bible nor ecclesiastical proscriptions have figured. His parents are conservative on the subject of sex, however, and they have urged Mark to maintain his virginity on the ground that it is "right," that is, a matter of fundamental principle, "natural law" being cited. Mark is under considerable pressure, both on a physiological and affectional basis and on a basis on conformity to the mores of his particular subculture, to indulge in a freer sexual expression. Apart from other considerations,[5] should he say No on a basis of natural law?

case 30. Honorable suicide?

Eugene Anderson has an incurable disease of protracted terminal character. He is considering fatally overdosing with barbiturates, for two reasons: there is fast being spent the savings needed for the care of his sole dependent, his wife; and means have not been found to reduce his continuing pain to the point where the joys of living outbalance it. Neither Church nor Bible have been norms for him, but of course he is aware of the general assumption that suicide is simply wrong. Would the natural law support his assumption? A serious survey of the matter has brought to his attention a few of the accepted practices in certain cultures, for example, the nationally endorsed valor of the Japanese kamikazes who dive-bombed to the decks of American ships; the Japanese custom of hara kiri as the accepted and only honorable "out" in certain circumstances; the equip-

[5] See pp. 130–31.

ping of certain spies of various nations with poison in order that upon capture they might avert the possibility of understandably revealing secrets under severe and protracted torture; the expected behavior (checked only recently) of Hindu wives in throwing themselves on the funeral pyres of their deceased husbands. Quite apart from the pros and the other cons applicable in his own situation, is the natural law an absolute con which should foreclose further consideration by Mr. Anderson?

case 31. Mercy for mothers?

Before the British House of Commons and before the California legislature are bills designed to extend the permissible grounds of abortion. At present in each jurisdiction abortion is permissible (with certain safeguards, such as the consent of the hospital's therapeutic abortion board) when it is adjudged that the mother's health, physical and mental, would be seriously impaired by continuation of the pregnancy. The new measures will allow similar relief in cases of pregnancy effected by rape or incest and in cases where it appears probable that an offspring of the pregnancy would suffer serious malformations, for example, because of the contraction of German measles by the mother in the course of her pregnancy.

In England the Episcopal members of the House of Lords are opposed *en banc;* in California two Episcopal dioceses are officially in favor, whereas the Roman Catholic bishops and the Missouri Synod Lutheran District are opposed. The opponents in each country make clear that they are not seeking to impose the teaching of their own respective Churches on the general populace; rather, they are upholding the natural law, which is applicable to all men. In the case of the Roman Catholic Church, the scope of the natural law in this regard is somewhat imprecise. St. Thomas Aquinas, St. Alphonus Liguori, and several popes have maintained that the fetus is not a human life until the time of "quickening"; other theologians have maintained that human life begins at the moment of conception. Medical opinion is similarly divided.

Those who hold the conception view and object to abortions under all or some circumstances call it murder and thus barred by the natural law. Many of the same people do not oppose capital punishment on the same grounds. If pressed they would draw a distinction: a felon who has been convicted of a capital crime is responsible for that which is his lot, whereas the innocent child who may suffer abortion has done no wrong. This in turn is answered by pointing out that, under enlightened criminology, we are not applying capital punishment to wreak vengeance on the defendant, but rather to deter capital crime (though as to the validity of this claim see CASE 10). A further distinction is to be observed: the Roman Catholic Church is also opposed to the existing law which allows therapeutic abortion when the life or health of the mother is at stake; the Church of England bishops condone abortion on this basis—though a "human life" is nevertheless taken, assuming the basis of their opposition to other grounds of abortion, namely, that the prequickening fetus is a person.

Should the current more limited laws be repealed? Should they be extended to include the additional grounds? And if so, how absolute is the principle of natural law which has been invoked?

case 32. Principle/platitude?

There are some long-recognized principles of natural law which really seem immune from the challenge of comparative or historical analysis. One of these is *suum cuique*, "To each according to his due." Mr. Walter Boyington, an aged widower, lived modestly but comfortably for some years before his demise on an ample pension which terminated at his death and did not provide for a beneficiary other than a spouse. He did, however, own a house situated on an extremely valuable commercial site. In looking through his papers after the funeral services were concluded his son Paul, a struggling businessman with a wife and four young children, found just three: a letter addressed to him, a deed to the property, recently drawn and properly recorded, with his father as grantor and his father and himself as grantees, tenants in common, and a properly drawn holographic last will and testament. On opening the letter he found that it contained his father's last loving thoughts, messages to be given to others and the request that Paul act as executor of his estate. In reading the will Paul found that the executor was charged with the payment of the last expenses; and that the property was bequeathed in varying and suitable proportions to the following persons: Mr. Boyington's brother; their infirm sister Agnes, a spinster, who also lived on a pension, though a much smaller one; Paul; Paul's wife; their four children; and finally, Mrs. Haverley, a middle-aged nurse-housekeeper who had devotedly and for very little recompense cared for Mr. Boyington at considerable sacrifice to herself. However sound or unsound, fair or unfair these various provisions may be, how helpful to the well-intentioned decedent in working it all out would be the natural law *suum cuique?*

Confusion has always attended the impressive phrase "natural law"; and its proponents have gained strength from the ambiguity. Natural law has been used to mean two things:

1. The body of principles and predictable operations discerned by the physical sciences through the use of the empirical or inductive method. It is thus used in these sentences—one pro and one contra conventional theology: it would be against the natural law for the stone to have rolled *itself* away on Easter morn; a virgin birth would be against the natural law.

2. A body of principles purportedly universal and eternal, which represent the norm of human behavior. It is thus used in the Cases above.

The first use has to do with *is's;* the second, with *oughts.* People who talk about natural law in the first sense don't always have their facts straight; people who talk about it in the second sense don't always have their norms straight. But in any case there is this marked difference in the two ways of using the same brief phrase.

Now people today have a profound respect for science. So when they hear something proclaimed as "natural law" they tend to attribute some of that respect to it—even though the affirmation is the spelling out of an *ought,* not *is.*

This is not a text on science or any branch of it. So we will not tarry to discuss (though it is an interesting topic for discussion) just how absolute scientific generalizations may or may not be. But it is important to note that whatever the answer to that question—the absoluteness of a pattern of *is's*—the question of the absoluteness of a pattern of *oughts* is a different subject.

It should be granted that, in theory, there is one point of

contact between the physical science natural law idea and the ethical natural law idea. Those who talk about natural law in the latter sense are operating, explicitly or implicitly, on the basis on this syllogism:

> *Major premise:*
> What mankind generally holds to be right or wrong is absolutely right or wrong.
> *Minor premise:*
> There are certain things mankind generally holds to be right or wrong.
> *Conclusion:*
> Therefore, these things are absolutely right or wrong.

Here we *seem* to be dealing in the minor premise with what *is*. But not really. Assuming that such universal conviction can be discerned on this point or that, still it is dealing at most with what lots of individuals think to be so—not directly with what is so.

But there is a fundamental difficulty with the *major premise*. Assume we could know at a given period in history what virtually everybody in the world approves of or disapproves of. Are ethics to be decided by a vote—even if it's a landslide? There have been periods when practically every nation or culture accepted slavery as right. Fifty years ago nearly all people, of whatever religion, regarded contraception as wrong. Does either fact have any logical relevance whatsoever to the question of the rightness of servitude or of family planning?

If the scope of credibility be limited to the views of more "advanced" peoples, would not all agree that Germany was an advanced culture at the time it tortured and cremated millions of Jews? Is it therefore part of the natural law that all Jews in sight be put to death? But it will be said, other advanced nations condemned that. Yes, but nevertheless the universality is hard to find. Further applying this test would make the current American policy of napalm-burning people alive in Vietnam absolutely wrong, since most of the people in well-nigh every other advanced nation (and unadvanced ones, too!) believe it to be wrong. It doubtless is wrong, but does the opinion of a vast majority of people in the world automatically make it so? If the universality of natural law is made evident through the study of wars and people's reaction to them, then why do not more Americans express outrage at our government's napalm policy?

The difficulty in finding universality is an obvious challenge to the *minor premise,* set out above. And there are two further difficulties with it. First, even if one could divine a general international consensus on a given point, could not the whole world be wrong and a *single* nonconformist right? Galileo is an obvious example—and, in the area of ethics as such, so was Margaret Sanger—or at least most people are coming to think so.

And that leads to the second difficulty: On what rational basis would one decide which is the normative century or decade, when history displays contradictory consensus? In the sixteenth and seventeenth centuries almost no one believed in religious liberty except for his own group (compare the Puritans' demand for freedom in England and their "righteous" denial of it to Baptists in Massachusetts). Denial of religious liberty was certainly practically universal and was believed to be right on the principle of *cuius regio, eius religio* and/or the principle that error has no rights. Now endorsement of the principle (though still lip service in some quarters) of religious freedom is virtually universal. The author and the readers doubtless prefer this latter posture. But the validity of natural law, insofar as it is supported on a basis of universal consensus, requires *immutability* as well as *universality*, because there is no rational device available to infallibilize the notions of any given period over those of any other.

To escape the withering effect upon the claim of natural law made by honest examination of history, some natural law exponents set forth only the most generic propositions. For example, *suum cuique*—to each his own, to each according to his due. This affirmation would doubtless meet both tests: universality as well as immutability—but at the cost of being a platitude! In any possible contest in which it would be called upon to supply the answer, the question would remain, What is whose own? What is each's due?

Or take a slightly more specific maxim: *Sic utere tuo ut alienum non laedas*—so use yours that you don't damage another. Sure. But open is the question how great must the likely damage to another be to block use? And another question: What special circumstances give one a right to use what he has to damage another? Can we use our napalm to burn their babies alive? Can we use our gas chamber to snuff out a convicted criminal's life? Can I use my nonzoned lot for a 44-story building to drive out the little corner grocer? The "natural law" gives us no answers to specific questions; and they—and they alone—are what matter.

In short: when "natural law" is specific it is not absolute; when it is unassailable it is platitudinous. It provides no platform for Code ethics. Nor do the Ten Commandments, New Testament texts, the teaching of the Church. A Code ethic is insupportable.

Two groups of people say that the only alternative is

antinomianism: no ethics. One group are Code ethicists who use this as a last ditch argument for their system. Another group use the fallacy of Code ethics as a basis for their support of freedom from ethics. They are convinced that the *ought* is thus demolished, that only the *is* remains.

Not many openly affirm no-ethics. Hence a chapter on it would seem to be taking on a straw man. But though it may have few explicit exponents, it is the working position of many individuals. So we turn to this position next.

chapter 6

NO ETHICS?

From the time a child is old enough to have discovered that he is often involved in situations in which his interests conflict with the interests of his playmates, parents, schoolteachers and those who people his world in general, the secret and cherished fantasy is born in him that some day—given power, riches, education, or possibly just enough courage—he can "do what he wants to do." Unless such a child discovers a more interesting image or comes under the sway of a logically or emotionally compelling system of ethics, he may reach adulthood determined to cannily live out this dream. If he has discovered the necessity of justifying his self-interested actions to a probably hostile circle of persons, he may call himself "antinomian" and trust that this polysyllablism will grant him some refuge from disapproval. But even if his neighbors, although writing off his conduct as selfish, do accept him, will the antinomist find that he has discovered the means to the ecstatic end of his reveries?

case 33. Eat her cake and have it too?

Geraldine Greene, a devout antinomist, has been told by her doctor that in order to prevent a disfiguring dermatitis caused by an allergy, from appearing on her face, she must avoid chocolate completely. Geraldine is concerned with her appearance but also enjoys eating, and finds chocolate particularly delicious. Her mother has prepared her favorite chocolate cake and invites her to have a piece. Can Geraldine do what she wants to do? What does she want to do?

case 34. Past, present, or future?

For some months, José Henderson has been unable to discharge an obligation incurred when he was ill and unable to work. His creditor has become unpleasantly demanding since José returned to full salary, and failure to pay the bill will soon mark him as a poor risk for obtaining credit in his home town. An elderly relative dies and leaves him a small bequest. José, although recovered, feels a holiday in a resort area he has long wanted to visit will restore him to his former buoyant self. At the same time a friend offers him an opportunity to invest in a small business that appears certain to be successful. The bequest is of such a size that José can spend the money in only one way. What will José, concerned with his own satisfaction, spend the money for? Will he obtain satisfaction?

case 35. What to say, oh, what shall I say?

The long-suffering wife of Joe Jackson has threatened to divorce him because of his many infidelities, and he feels that she is certain to obtain a disastrously large financial settlement. He has long been unhappy with her, and has become deeply involved with Karen Knutson. Although he realizes that Karen cares a great deal for the financial security he can give her, he believes that she also loves him. At an office party Joe becomes attracted to another young woman, one who is gay and unescorted. Believing in doing what he wants to do, he invites her to spend the night in the city with him. The next morning he learns from a friend at the office that the young woman is well acquainted with both his wife and Miss Knutson and is the type who will undoubtedly tell them of her amorous adventures of the night before. As an antinomist of some experience Joe has faith in, and no compunction about, lying. But to whom should he lie? Will it work?

Without belaboring the obvious mutual exclusivity, from a semantic point of view, of antinomianism and "ethics," it is possible to engage with the picture of an adroit, adept, and possibly athletic antinomist who is able to stay ahead of an outraged group of friends, relatives, and acquaintances, and examine antinomianism on its own terms in the search for a meaningful criterion for choosing an ethical point of view.

It is not unthinkable to picture three sorts of men, with appropriately attendant conditions for whom antinomianism might be, or seem to be, a satisfactory style of life: the hermit, the psychotic, and the agile person described above. Almost anyone else would soon run into the stone wall of societal disapproval with its attendant restrictions, or would be in the unhappy position of having to conform to some workable—for him—system of ethics while enduring the constant frustration of his averred plan for living. We will for the sake of the argument, postulate a hermit in the United States.

case 36. If I could only be alone!

Larry Livingston is a young man who has spent considerable time in introspection. As a result of self-analysis, he realizes the following things: he does not like to work, he finds living with relatives irksome, jail or other institutions are odious to him, being a beggar or "con artist" involves the display of attitudes toward others that he prefers not to show, and he finds all welfare investigators repugnant. He has no available money and no prospects for winning a contest or becoming an heir. His quite passionately held creed is antinomian. He decides to become a hermit. Where will he go? How will he obtain food and shelter?

case 37. Asylum for freedom?

A young woman, Julie Larson, also realizes that she, like Larry, cannot—or really will not—obtain sufficient money for her material needs. Unlike Larry she does not desire to become an anchorite, although she does not wish to live in intimate relationship with anyone either. Rather than abandon her I-do-what-I-want-to-do position, after appraising the possibilities, she decides to feign mental illness and thus be fed and housed without responsibility for anything or anybody—and without being expected to relate sensitively to people. Is Julie's antinomian stance vindicated by this action?

Certainly one is tempted to dispose of the antinomian position at this point by resorting to that crisp and immensely satisfying phrase of undergraduate days, "absurd in theory and impossible in practice." But we have yet to contend with that almost unimaginable person who is able skillfully both to overcome all objections to his behavior and also to evade all the results of it.

When the pronouncements of the antinomists are carefully analyzed, it becomes evident that there is often an unverbalized (perhaps even denied) prepositional ending to the sentence, "I do what I want to do . . ." More often than not such a person does have a norm for his conduct, or at least some criterion of greater preference to which he instinctively subjects his choices; that is, "I do what I want to do for pleasure," or ". . . for excitement," or ". . . for future gain," or ". . . for comfort," or ". . . for aggrandizement," or for whatever kind of self-satisfaction to which his psyche has conditioned him.

To the degree that he recognizes that one or more of these criteria are operative, to that degree a kind of self-ontology is discovered by one who thinks he has disposed of all absolution.

Without plumbing the deeps of clinical psychology it is easy to see that many "I's"—different ones at different times—can exist simultaneously under the cover of an ongoing sense of identity. There is the self of yesterday, today, tomorrow, as well as the self of five minutes from now. As we saw in CASE 33, *Eat her cake and have it too?* Geraldine was faced with an uncomfortable decision because she desired two things that were incompatible. Should she indulge her desire of the moment or plan for her desire of tomorrow? The antinomist here is forced by the circumstances of her body to make an evaluative decision that destroys the logical base of her position—that she does what she wants to do.

There are facets of the self which may suffer considerably if one element of the personality is indulged indiscriminately and these in a vicious, circular way make the appeasement of the original craving difficult. This was evident in CASE 34, *Past, present, or future,* and more than likely would be true in the story of the too-many-ladied lover of CASE 35. Self-interest in isolation is a difficult concept with which to engage, and the seeker of it to the exclusion of all else is in an unenviable position.

Sooner or later a further disquietude will disturb the antinomist—one which finally demolishes his position if he can bring himself to to look at it.

case 38. Whose ox is being gored?

At 2 A.M. Bill, an 007 type, had just left Sue's apartment. For a couple of weeks now he'd wanted her as another notch in his belt. Once would be enough. His alert eyes had already spotted three more he wanted to make. He had built it up a lot, telling her he loved her, that they had a great future. Four or five drinks (he always stayed fairly sober himself) to soften her up. It worked. It usually did. He wasn't coming back—*fait accompli.* What about *her?* That's her problem. He started his car, pulled out. Another car doing sixty down the side street ripped off his fender. He was furious and damned the careless driver. Why should he have? The next day he learned that an incompetent nephew of the boss got the job his good work had created. His resentment knew no bounds. Why should he have been resentful?

case 39. Not game for wife-swapping

Late in a bacchanalian party, Joe suggested to Sally, whom he'd met that night, that they drift off to a bedroom for a quiet talk. Their talk was brief: one question and one answer. "Is it wrong?" "Not if we want each other tonight."

They did. An hour later they went back down the hall to rejoin the crowd. En route Joe opened a door, thinking it was the bathroom, and saw his wife in bed with Sally's husband. He emitted a value-charged word, and he gave Sally's husband a black eye. Why?

In each case there is, at the least, inconsistency. It can be argued that this widespread human foible of being inconsistent proves nothing, but it's a pretty snarly and consistent inconsistency. Part of the data of reality is the plain fact that virtually everybody feels a sense of right and wrong when he's the object of something he doesn't like. He utters judgmental labels, defends his "rights," feels bound up, and in general protests—and protests vehemently. Whether in each instance he is justified in his instinctive reaction in the light of an avowed no-ethic, it is there. And this datum of experience displays a well-nigh universal instinct that there is a right—or rightful—dimension in human behavior. Practically no one is relaxed about the *is* when outrageous things are done to him. In fact, this pervasive feeling of rightness is, empirically speaking, part of the *is*. Is this just social conditioning? No, it's too deep and ineradicable. Not social conditioning; rather, vice versa. It is not just an effect; it's the root cause of much social conditioning, both bad and good.

Even though it can be shown that there is no logical base for the antinomian position, even though the incongruity of the living out of no-lawism verges on the absurd—nevertheless, it is the disquietude we have been discussing that can finally reduce the antinomist to the unhappy awareness that his stance is impossible.

We can now state this disquietude.

The antinomist has discovered that there are other antinomists in his world.

chapter 7

THINGS AND PERSONS

case 40. The line is drawn

The New Age Chemical Corporation is eager to measure the solvent properties of a newly created organic compound. The first tests are with hard rubber, the next with various formerly insoluble salts, then with the branches from green saplings. After this, the corrosive substance is applied to the skin of rats. This is sufficiently successful for the next step intended, that of injecting the fluid into their bloodstreams, to be canceled as unnecessary. Each phase of the experiment is carefully noted and a straight line graph plotted with the amount of solvent required and the degree of destruction as coordinates. To finish up the project it is decided to try out the compound on employees. The union enters the scene. They have not been concerned about the first three portions of the experiment, the rubber, salts, and trees; nor have they moved to protect the rats. The Anti-Vivisection Society did, but few employees or members of the public were interested. Why a fervid objection now?

case 41. "I'll talk"

A teller, about to close his desk, is alone in a small rural bank. The last customer turns out to be a hold-up man. At gunpoint the teller is ordered to tell where the money is. He does and the thief makes away with about $4,000. The chief cashier insists on firing the teller, but the president refuses.

The fact that these cases are absurd and their outcomes obvious quickly leads us to our first positive point in discerning a viable ethic. Everyone knows empirically that persons are different from other items of reality, whatever his view of physiology, psychology, or human destiny.

In CASE 40, *The line is drawn,* persons in general (not just members of the union's grievance committee) are protected; in CASE 41, *"I'll talk,"* the teller protected himself. Self-preservation has been rated as the primary human instinct; and the validity of the instinct and the rightness of acting it out is universally recognized. Self is viewed here generically. Hence, it is a legitimate inference that other selves (other than the one self at the moment engaged in self-preservation) are valuable too.

Persons are more important than things.

William Hazlitt has reminded us that man is the only animal that can laugh or weep. And why? Because he is the only animal which can discern the difference between the way things are and the way they ought to be. Man transcends the *is;* he can take thought and change it. He transcends the *now.* He ties past, present, and future together: he can reflect on the latter, learn from it (both +'s and —'s) and anticipate the future, laying foundations for +'s and protection against —'s. Contrary to Matt. 6:34, he does take thought for the morrow. He can, within limits (narrower than we used to think before Freud), make decisions—and implement them in short- and long-term ways. He can communicate, not only facts but notions. He can, in a measure, reveal himself to others and grasp, in a measure, what others reveal of themselves. All this is empirical data, not just a prefab theological dogma.

case 42. Meddler/man for others

A group of Negroes have organized a peaceful demonstration in a Southern town in which by various devices their right to vote has been almost universally denied. They are bullwhipped and subjected to tear gas by the police. The latter then form a cordon around the Negro ghetto. Milling around behind are many hostile white people, shouting epithets and threats; some are armed.

With full knowledge of the situation, Jim, a minister from New England, joins hundreds of other clergy going to the town to be alongside the Negroes as they plan and undertake their next peaceful demonstration. On emerging from a local coffee shop, he is shot and killed by an angry local white citizen (who, as is the custom in the region, is acquitted on his trial). The incident receives international news coverage through the mass media. What motive or motives could have gotten Jim into his risky business? What would be the likely responses to Jim's action on the part of the readers, viewers, and listeners?

case 43. Twelfth step

After losing the two previous nights' sleep, one with a sick mother and one in travel, Dave turned in at 9, planning to sleep until 6:30, when he had to get up to go to work. At 11:15, he got a call from Bud, fellow member of the local chapter of A.A. Bud was sinking into a depression and did not trust himself to hold out from the bottle much longer. Without hesitation Dave said he'd be there as soon as he could get there. He knew, from past experiences with what in the movement is called "twelfth-step" work, that there was immediate therapy in that promise and that Bud would doubtless stay dry until he could dress, drive an hour, and get there. He was right. After drinking coffee with Bud and listening a great deal and talking some, at 2:30 Dave felt he could safely leave; he went home and got to sleep at 4 A.M. "Tonight, I'll catch up," he thought. Why did Dave take on this task when he was all that bushed? What would be the likely response of others who might hear about it?

case 44. No step

Two months later, Dave was about to leave the house for a "late date" at May's apartment. She is a promiscuous girl with whom he had sex from time to time; neither had any serious interest in each other. He planned to stay all night since it would be more convenient to go direct from there to the office in the morning. The phone rung. It was Gertrude, an in-and-out older member of his A.A. group. She'd started to drink that evening, but wanted to stop. Would he come over? She lived quite a distance from downtown. He hesitated, knowing that May would be there—and "available"—any time he arrived (she didn't take her sleep very seriously). But he was tired—and also eager: because of work pressures he had been a celibate for a while. So he spent five minutes on the phone with Gertrude hastily emitting platitudes, then told her that he wished he could come out but that he was late meeting a plane on which an important customer was arriving. Then he went downtown. He learned later that Gertrude had tried a couple of other members, both away from home, drinking as she continued to seek help, and that she had then decided (or, more likely, by this time she was unable to make a decision) to go right on drinking. She continued for four days, meanwhile losing her job.

A bit later, on a plane, Dave got to thinking about himself. It was nothing as formal as an examination of conscience—just an informal self-analysis. Among the items he reviewed were the experiences in this and the previous Case. What would be his probable estimates of his motives on each occasion? What light would the contrast between them throw on his own image of himself?

At the end of each Case two quite different questions are asked. The first in each pair has to do with the inner situation of the man with whom we are concerned. The second has to do with the response of others (or, in the last Case, of the person himself) to the image the particular episode presents. It is the latter which is relevant at this point in our analysis. For simplification let us specify and drop out of consideration one "minority report" on Jim's action and the outcome in CASE 42, *Meddler/man for others.* To racists and some other conservatives—in the North as well as in the South—the reactions[1] ranged from "He deserved what he got" to "Too bad, but if he'd stuck to preaching and not pushed his nose into something that was none of

[1] This is in the indicative not the subjunctive because it is obvious the facts are based on the murder of the Rev. James Reeb, Unitarian minister slain in Selma, Alabama (incidentally, the same day the author was there).

his business he'd be alive today." But here is exemplified a category of response reflective of a high degree of social conditioning, or a very rigid if not paranoid personality type, or a high priority on specific interests—real or supposed—the given respondent may have had in maintenance of white supremacy.

Leaving out then this special and atypical response to the situation in CASE 42, there are two typical responses to the situations in both this Case and 43, *Twelfth step*. Which of the two emerges tells us a good deal about the reactor. The first is that of the "007" type: "Tough. But what was there in it for him?" To persons like this, Jim rushing to Selma or David rushing to his fellow alcoholic is equally ridiculous and as to the outcome (Jim's death and David's exhaustion): "Well, that just shows you!"

But apparently much more widespread would be another type of response: shock and distress in the case of Jim, admiration for both Jim and Dave (the "twelfth step" Dave, not the "no step" Dave). A third reaction, which is widespread enough to provide a second category of data (alongside of the sensing of the differences between persons and things, taken up at the start of this chapter). This second category, like the first, is supportive of an affirmation of positive ethics.

Many, many people (probably most people) when they see or hear of a marked instance of someone's outgoingness to others are touched, even moved—mysteriously having a warm feeling inside. There is a genuine joy in the very fact that such a thing can be displayed by people. It is *self-authenticating* goodness. What kind of manifestation elicits this spontaneous response?

Socrates' stance, as reflected in his reported addresses at various stages of his heresy trial, shows no trimming for safety's sake. Instead, he shows confidence in his cause (against idolatry, for "the only wise God"[2]), forgiveness of his accusers and judges, and trust in the future—post-hemlock.

The words and actions reported of Jesus in His closing days reflect an image of One (to make a paraphrase which St. Paul's summary in Philippians 2 tolerates) who emptied himself of success—or status-concern, didn't care about reputation (or any other idol), assumed the role of the Man for Others,[3] and to the very end was obedient to His calling and His unflinching witness against the religious and political Establishment.

In all these great human moments there shows through a quality that evokes, in thousands and millions, an intuitive response. How define it? The author has been looking for a single word for it for a couple of years, but in vain. The best he can do is the conflation of three words, recognizing that the quantity of what is pointed to by each varies in each instance and yet sensing that what is suggested by the multiple designation is at bottom really one quality: TRUTH-COURAGE-LOVE.

Since our approach does not use or seek to find an ontological or authority basis for meaning, our focus at this point is not on the abstract value of this quality but rather on the empirical fact.[4] Thus we can permit a generic to stand for the response to the manifestations of truth-courage-love wherever seen. And this is true not only of the vivid images of notables recognized in different cultures throughout the centuries, but also of contemporary ex-

[2] Cf. 1 Tim. 1:17.

[3] Dietrich Bonhoeffer, *Letters and Papers from Prison* (New York: The Macmillan Company, 1962), pp. 179–80.

[4] See chap. 6.

amples more directly experienced. When we see this in others a lot of us like it. It makes no difference if the goodness is directed toward ourselves or others. More than that, generally when a man sees such goodness in himself, with more or less frequency, he likes it. CASES 43-44, *Twelfth step/No step,* illustrate this. From the few facts, it would appear highly likely that David, in retrospect, would like himself better for the hours of his life spent alongside Bud than for the hours during which he failed to meet Gertrude's urgent need. Granted, during this time his recreation with May was more pleasant than the patient sitting with Gertrude would have been. But the happening was now long over—and in fact mattered little two minutes after he'd turned over to go to sleep (one of the characteristics of casual sex, as compared with sex with an abiding love and involvement). It is highly likely that David, during the reflection on the plane, liked the CASE-43 David better than the CASE-44 David.

We are now ready to sum up the data that could lead to an affirmation as to a style of life:

a. The observably empirical fact that persons are different from things—a difference of more significance and value than inheres in any other distinction.
b. The widespread intuitive and spontaneous response of healthy-minded persons to conspicuous examples of concern for others.
c. A similar response to clear individual reaction to this kind of acting from time to time, whether on the part of others or of ourselves.

These are facts, not theories or ideals or hopes. It is not too immodest an inference from the great body of data in these three categories to affirm—granted, by faith not proof—that the Man for Others style of life is the best norm.

This moving and apt phrase, more and more in use since Pastor Bonhoeffer coined it and Bishop John Robinson even more widely popularized it,[5] is generally uttered as "man for *others*." But this well-meaning emphasis plays down an equally important half of the norm, signified by the first word of the phrase. All the data outlined above support a high valuation of the first noun as much as they support a high valuation of the second noun coupled with the directional preposition. The reason we should serve the *other* is that he is a *man*. The fulfillment of the *servant* is as important as the fulfillment of the *served*. We should not treat persons as things is clear from all that has been said. To minimize the personhood of the man who is to be "for others" is to view him as an object—simply as a means to serve another end, that is, as a thing. The ancient love of others commandment puts it right: "Thou shalt love thy neighbor as thy *self*."

So the self, the serving self, is of no less value than anyone being served. Available are particularly relevant data to support this affirmation and also to show, too, that the two values are not necessarily in conflict—as often as a choice between the two is required at particular moments of decision-making.

case 45. Blind leading the blind

Let's assume that David is himself in-and-out in his A.A. attendance because he has frequently fallen off the wagon. One time when Bud urgently called for help, even in his condition he could not fail to notice that David was more incomprehensible on his end of the phone than Bud was on his. One time when he did go to Gertrude's side, little

[5] In his *Honest to God* (Philadelphia: Westminster Press, 1963), chap. 4.

conviction was carried because Gertrude herself had been at meetings David missed—when it had been indicated he had tied one on. Under these circumstances how much help is he to those "others"?

case 46. For/against

Margaret doesn't know the word "No" when it comes to accepting calls to join committees and projects that serve the community. She has gotten into a perpetual state of exhaustion and less and less does she come through with tasks undertaken. Her past record of dedicated involvement over the years has made her co-workers in any of the groups reticent to suggest she drop out of some things. Cannot the *for* in the three-word phrase, while still strong in intention, weaken in reality? Cannot it even become *against?*

case 47. Self-serving service

A characteristic distortion in A.A. testimony is reflected in such statements as "In doing twelfth-step work I'm being selfish: it helps me stay dry." If this really told the whole story it would be "using" people—treating them as things, even though it might well be to their benefit. And generally it is only a *half*-truth: the alcoholic thus serving does in fact rejoice in the fact that he is thus helping bring recovery to others. But isn't it this "selfish" remark a half-*truth?* His own degree of health (more specifically his maintenance of sobriety) is reinforced in his direct work with others.

The point doesn't need to be spelled out. The healthy, whole, fulfilled person has more to help others with; the more we help others the more healthy, whole, and fulfilled we become and are.

The model of goodness is self-authenticating: *fulfilled* and *other-directed.*

The likelihood of all this taking place depends not just on the outward fact but on the inward dynamics, namely, motive. As important as what we do is why we do it. Why be good, why do good? This we consider next.

case 48. Quid pro quo

Brian Olsen was the closest living relative of his childless and elderly uncle, William Olsen. It occurred to Brian, at the time of the death of his aunt, that he would be the logical heir to his uncle's estate. But he also realized that the latter had a few more distant relatives who kept in touch from time to time with his uncle. Brian had for years given the old man hardly more than an occasional telephone call, even though he lived in the same part of town. So he feared that he might not be included in Uncle William's will.

Brian began to call on his uncle at the time of his aunt's death. He found his talks with his uncle very boring (the latter was lengthy and repetitious in his ruminating) and the whole experience was quite tedious. But Brian never let his actual reaction show, and the new and increasing attentiveness from his nephew brought something quite sustaining into William's life. So, good rather than evil has come the uncle's way. Is Brian's new activity ethical?

case 49. Fire insurance

Priscilla believes that if she sins and should happen to die before repenting, she will spend all eternity in hell. Conjoined with this belief is a conviction that every good deed she does over and above the Code helps counterbalance the punishment (in this world or the next) due for sins already repented of. Accordingly she studiously avoids doing anything she regards as sinful and engages in "extra" good works as frequently as she has opportunity. How ethical is she in these various restraints and actions?

In consideration of these Cases let us also consider again CASE 47, *Self-serving service*, assuming for present purposes that the given recovered alcoholic, whom we will call Matt, is truly reflecting the extent of his inner motive when he protests that he helps other alcoholics only because it helps him keep dry. Now in each of these three Cases we can assume that the actual objective results are good. How good is the motive? In no one of the three Cases is the activity necessarily *un*ethical. Harm is not being done another, indeed good is. In fact if the hypothesis of the actor in each Case be granted, good results both for the actor and for the other or others involved.

In CASE 48, *Quid pro quo*, if Brian does inherit, to a certain degree he will have earned it—especially if his uncle lives a long time. The uncle will have had something his latter years which will have been quite important to him—and hard to buy.

In CASE 47, *Self-serving service*, the alcoholics reached out to, on a basis of the twelfth step, received precisely the kind of help which experience shows is the most likely to effect recovery.

Furthermore, it was for nothing in comparison to psychiatric help, which in the case of alcoholism is much less likely to be successful. And as for Priscilla's studied inactions and actions (CASE 49, *Fire insurance*) some people are not being hurt that might otherwise be, and some people are being benefited that might not otherwise be.

If morality (old or new) had only to do with objective acts or restraints and their good or evil character, we could simply label what is involved in these Cases as "ethical" and let it go at that. But this external view would be contrary to a motif we have already endorsed: it would be to view persons as things. One of the most predominant aspects of our ever more rapidly changing culture is the speedy increase of items that are the work of machines rather than the direct work of persons. When a beverage dispenser at the push of the right button and the deposit of a dime turns out coffee with sugar but without cream or when a computer turns out the right answer to a complicated problem, we might call the machine efficient, but it would never occur to us to call it ethical (nor, incidentally, if the wrong mix were poured out or an erroneous answer delivered, would we call the machine unethical). So ethics has to do not only with *what* a person does or does not do, but also with *why* he does or doesn't do something.

Therefore, it is appropriate that we turn to the motive in these last Cases. While, as we shall shortly see, a mark of human finitude is our incapacity to make accurate judgments as to other people's motives (or even as to our own), nevertheless motive as such is an important component of ethical behavior.

It is in order to be able to say something about this element that the Cases have been deliberately overdrawn.

Many who would have no difficulty in seeing Brian's and Matt's motive as simply self-interest would not so readily perceive that Priscilla's is also. Doing something for the purpose of gaining personal advantage or refraining from something to avert personal disadvantage is generally labeled as "self-seeking" or "self-regarding" when the outcome sought to be achieved or avoided falls within the earthly time span; but when the dating of the outcome is in the life to come the action or inaction is rated as "religious," hence good. Logically the difference lies only in the short-range or long-range (relatively speaking) nature of the expectations. Matt expects almost immediate good, namely, support for his own sobriety, from his efforts in helping another alcoholic recover; Brian expects good in a few years, namely, the proceeds of his aged uncle's estate, from his sustained attentiveness; Priscilla, by her sacrifices in her earthly years, is laying a foundation for eternal bliss.

When put this candid way, the point is easy enough to see. That it has not been generally seen is owing to the fact that, with some modification in some quarters in the present era, the Churches have strongly emphasized the connection of earthly behavior with rewards and punishments in the hereafter. And in this they have had no less a Biblical basis than the Sermon on the Mount. For example:

> Blessed are ye, when men shall revile you, and persecute you and say all manner of evil against you falsely for my sake. Rejoice, and be exceeding glad: for great is your reward in heaven. (Matt. 5:11-12, AV)

> . . . whosoever is angry with his brother without a cause shall be in danger of the judgment: . . . (22a)

> . . . whosoever shall say, Thou fool, shall be in danger of hell fire. (22c)

> And if thy right eye offend thee, pluck it out, and cast it from thee: for it is profitable for thee that one of thy members should perish, and not that thy whole body should be cast into hell. (29)

> Love your enemies, . . . for if ye love them which love you what reward have ye? (44a, 46a)

Take heed that ye do not your alms before men, to be seen of them; otherwise ye have no reward of your father which is in heaven. (6:1)

For if ye forgive men their trespasses, your heavenly Father will also forgive you: but if ye forgive not men their trespasses, neither will your Father forgive your trespasses. (14-15)

The fact that the Churches, with no less formidable support than such texts, have placed such emphasis on other-world sanctions, has sanctified this long-range form of the self-serving motive for doing good and eschewing evil. Viewed as "religious" and "holy" is what in the most favorable context is prudence. In the least favorable context it is selfishness.

Now that we have all three actors grouped in the same category, it is appropriate to ask the question, Do we have here an ethical motive? In seeking to answer the question, we should eliminate from consideration the soundness—on factual or theological grounds—of the given expectation. Maybe on one of his late evening twelfth-step calls Matt may end up helping finish the bottle; upon his uncle's death Brian may discover to his dismay that his uncle has left everything to the S.P.C.A.; Priscilla after death may discover that there is not a clear dichotomy between heaven and hell, and that where one is in the scene is not based on bookkeeping as to good and evil deeds but on what she has become—and will be becoming—as a person in terms of freedom, openness to the new, and capacity to love and be loved. But whether people's genuine expectations are soundly or unsoundly grounded, we can only evaluate motive in the light of the expectations they in fact have. Each of our characters believes he is acting in his own best interests.

We have already affirmed above, in analyzing the Man

for Others model, that since the reason the other is to be served is that he is a person, for precisely the same reason the fulfillment of self is a proper aim. Where the pursuing of the same appears to be in conflict with the need of another, one is not called upon automatically to say No to self-interest and Yes to the interest of the other. The same kind of weighing is involved as in the case of a decision one might have to make as to *which* of two others to serve when the needs of both cannot be adequately met under the circumstances. But in the CASES we have been considering there is apparent no such conflict of interests; quite to the contrary, the interests of the other parties were being served too—even though, the way the CASES are stated, service was not the motive. So the situations are not different in principle from ones in which no other person is directly involved. If a man decides to use free time to go to a gym and take a workout, either for physical benefit or for enjoyment (or for both), he is operating on a good ethical motive, whether he thinks of the matter in ethical terms or not.

But the fact is that in the Cases at hand others *are* involved. And each configuration is such that there is a relevant place for the motive of service to others. As we have seen, the existence of a self-serving motive is not in itself bad, or even neutral: it is in itself a positive ethical motive. The ethical negative in our Cases lies in the fact that in relationships where there is room for the outgoing motive, its lack denies to both giver and receiver that which love brings to any situation. Each falls short of the Man for Others model in what is clearly a potential example of this very model. The normal negative or neutral reaction points to the conclusion that self-interest is not an adequate motivation even though others are being served—in fact *be-*

cause they are being served.

This brings us to the most fundamental consideration. Why, when less is good and more is better, is the latter called for? Why is the most possible from us called for? Why the greatest possible personal fulfillment and the greatest possible service to others? It is hoped that there has been provided earlier in the chapter an answer grounded in empirical data. For those who are by conviction nontheistic no more can be said. Is there more to say from a theistic premise? If one believes in an ultimate Ground of reality, the relevance of such a belief to the decision-making of life is vital. "Truth is in order to goodness."

Contrary to the impression of many Christians, each of the two "great commandments" is found in the Old Testament:

> Hear, O Israel: The Lord our God is one Lord; and you shall love the Lord your God with all your heart, and with all your soul, and with all your might. (Deut. 6:4-5)

> . . . you shall love your neighbor as yourself . . . (Lev. 19:18b)

The contribution of the New Testament is the linking of the two together and the precise way they are linked: "The second is like it" (Mark 12: 29-30).

To see what the apparently simple phrase "like it" means, we need to notice the connection between the two parts of the first great commandment. The first sentence sounds like theology, the second like a special law—one (among many) issued by the Subject of the first sentence. Actually, the second affirmation is *entailed* by the first—logically required by it.

If it be affirmed that there is but one Ultimate, then human response and human decision-making is freed from bondage to any of a variety of pseudo-ultimates. There are not a number of final claims. Hence, *all* your heart, *all* your mind, *all* your soul, *all* your strength. There is only One of Him; hence He can claim all. No one else, nothing else can have the last word on any portion of one's life. No other person: no one in everyday life, no "authority," civil or ecclesiastical. No thing, whether a material object or an abstract principle, no personal or historical goal or objective, no item of human code. This is the negative, iconoclastic impact.

The positive point is man's total responsibility. Insofar as he is free, man is called, in all realms, to make decisions responsibly. But to what end? Where man finds himself, a unique individual in society with others, this "whole" response must be in reference to what is happening—and can happen—to himself and to others personally known and unknown—on which his decisions have a bearing: in short, self and neighbor. And the latter word is not a restrictive one in terms of category, it is restrictive only in terms of opportunity. The lawyer asked an abstract—or code—question: "Who is my neighbor?" The Parable of the Good Samaritan ends with an existential question: "Who was neighbor to the man who fell among thieves?"[6]

So just as the totality of the claim is entailed in the "*one* Lord" affirmation, the fulfillment of self and service of others is entailed by the claim. So, the *second is like it*.

The word "love" is used in both. "Like it" applies here too. The quality or kind of love is meant to be the same. What it is can best be perceived by considering what is the most adequate form of love of others, "for he who does not love his brother whom he has seen cannot love God whom he has not seen" (1 John 4:20b).

[6] See Esther Pike, *Who Is My Neighbor?* (New York: Seabury Press, 1960), chap. 1.

chapter 8

WHAT PRESERVES PERSONS?

case 50. Love-starved

Mary thoroughly rejects her child because he is the son of a husband who deserted her for a younger woman and whom she hates—deeply and implacably. She has lacked courage either to kill the boy or starve him; in fact, by a strange twist of conscience, has made every physical provision for his welfare. But no affection comes through from her to her son, and whenever she has seen affection shown to him by any relative or friend she has quickly blocked them from him. The child grows more and more ill and dies in his sleep. Why?

case 51. Phony love

Flora's widowed mother has only a limited income, and there seems nothing to do but move her into Flora's small apartment. All her adult life Flora has been irked by her mother's demands. She feels no attraction to her, respects few of her ideas, but feels that her real duty requires the new living arrangement. Flora sees to it that the older woman has a reasonable amount of necessities and comforts, arranges that she never be left alone at night, and when they are together forces herself to enter into conversation and keep up a cheery atmosphere. This she sees as the demand of Christian love. Yet her mother is laden with a deep and sad sense of bereavement, and Flora is constantly aware of an uncomfortable burden—though a burden courageously borne. What's wrong here?

case 52. A "no-good whore"

Tom Driver, a probation officer, is interviewing a prostitute on probation. He regards her whole mode of life as distasteful, not only her professional activities, but her limited outlook, her vulgarity of dress and inappropriateness of make-up. He cringes at her strident voice, her shallow personality, her slinky figure, her general gaucherie. There seems to be nothing he can find to like about her. But devising a more constructive program for her and inspiring her to follow it is what he is paid for—besides, he has in mind what his minister has so often said: "You don't have to like, you're supposed to love; and Christian love (*agapē*) requires no feeling for or appreciation of the other person. It means accepting him as a person and seeking to meet his need." This he is doing. Is it enough? She knows. And nothing enriches him from the encounter.

Merely to be alive requires a lot of things; really to be alive and whole requires love: loving and being loved. This is not just a principle derived from higher authority; it is a fact observable everywhere and every day. Dr. Smiley Blanton's book title says half of it: *Love or Perish*. A sequel could be entitled *Be Loved or Perish*. Here is an essential of well-being. It is scientifically verifiable. A straight materialistic internist skilled in psychosomatic medicine can see it; the secularist psychiatrist can see it.

Facts in the real world around us, not authoritative laws imposed from the outside, are these: persons count more than things; the well-being of persons requires certain conditions. Some of these conditions can be brought about by self-help, some by mutual arrangement, some by the gift of others. The fullest gifts and the most wholesome way of giving—for donor and receiver—is *love.*

But love is a fuzzy word. What kind of love? More and more familiar is the distinction between *erōs*, *philia,* and *agapē*. Hence the following definitions are not meant as an analysis of the three kinds of love, but as a reminder before we confront the crucial question, "What kind of love?"

Erōs is the love of the lovable; the object of the loving is the source of it.

Philia is the affection which arises between people because of mutual interest or focus; an outside factor is its source.

Agapē is the love of the apparently unlovable.[1] Its source is in the one loving—from duty, or in response to being so loved by God or man.

Christian moral theologians, basing their view on New Testament texts, give *agapē* the highest marks.[2] Code ethicists include the requirement of it among the rules, some proponents of the new morality set it forth as the sole

[1] Professor Joseph Fletcher says: "We can say quite plainly and colloquially that Christian love is the business of loving the unlovable, i.e., the *unlikable*" in his *Situation Ethics* (Philadelphia: Westminster Press, 1966), p. 105.

[2] E.g., Fletcher, *op. cit.*, p. 49; and the author's *Doing the Truth*, pp. 131 ff., *The Next Day* (New York: Doubleday & Company, Inc., 1957), chap. 8.

ethic. *But it is not the best brand of love, either for the lover or loved.* It is not enough.

Take the Cases. The deprived child was not denied *agapē*. His situation met the definition. He was (to his mother) unlovable and his every need was met, except one—the need to be responded to as lovable. He died—showered with *agapē*. And his mother, as shown by the very fact that his death was no loss to her, had lost an opportunity to be a whole person. Similarly, Flora's mother, agapēized, is deprived of *the* healing thing, and Flora is carrying what is a sheer burden. The prostitute, though given the appropriate fruits of *agapē*, is not furnished any appreciation of herself as a person. Her not being loved for herself is central to her problem. And the caseworker was deprived of the expression of the best thing he had (if he had it)—the capacity for love, with appreciation of a new and unique person. All are losers.

Agapē is treating persons as things. It's better to meet the material needs of persons than not to meet any needs. (Presumably it was better that Mary feed her son than that she not—though in the end it didn't make much difference.) But *eros* is the fullness of what we're capable of giving and the richest gift to receive. Again, this is fact, not law; experience, not principle.

But it has been said that *erōs* can't be commanded; *agapē* can. We are to love (agapēistically) people we don't like. What can be achieved by command and what is the good, however, are not the same thing. *Agapē* is not only not the full good; it partakes of evil. In its "pure" form, without admixture of *erōs* or *philia,* it is a "putting down" of the person thus "loved."[3] It supplies a sense of goodness

[3] Dr. Fletcher says, *op. cit.,* "Pinned down to his precise meaning, Christian love is benevolence, literally."

and well-doing to one person while belittling the other. For it to be recognizably operative it is intrinsically requisite that the other be assessed as unlovable, unworthy, undeserving, *no good.*

Whatever specific immediate needs of the agapēized one are being met and however well they are being met, the deepest need—to be respected as a person—is not only *not* being met, it is being intensified.

But the supporters of *agapē* as the highest love—and they are legion, including both the conventional and the situation ethicist—would answer that part of the *agapē* package by recommending the concealment of this write-off, this disrespect, out of concern for the other person. There are two difficulties with this:

1. This would mean that hypocrisy is built in—is part of the very nature of *agapē*. To tell the truth presents a different problem from making an existential decision, where all the factors are weighed in a given context, as in CASE 13, *Lying—but patriotically*. Dishonesty is inherent in full *agapē*. Thus there are harmful effects on the actor: habituation to deceit, increase of resentment—hidden or open, and diminution of a posture of candor in life.

2. The feigned liking of another is not uniformly successful, especially in relationships which are ongoing if for even a short time. Respectful words and even responsive action, however carefully designed, do not always successfully hide the basic disrespect, the inner estimate that there is nothing in the other worth responding to. Even when there is the best possible "cover," the one on the receiving end of *agapē*, whether by intuition or extra-sensory perception, or because of perceiving occasional cracks in the cover, can *know*. And when he does know, there is resultant humiliation, sense of inferiority, and resentment—all

of which can combine to increase his apparent unlovability.

In being realistic about these factors, we do not mean to overstate the case. The plain fact is that there are many, many encounters in which a person with particular needs does not in any way attract the person or persons equipped to meet those needs. And the needs ought to be met. Meeting needs is the exercise of positive ethics and to that extent *agapē* is a good thing. But obviously it is not good enough.

chapter 9

BEYOND *AGAPĒ*

case 53. Love-starved, revisited

Mary, in CASE 50, was so consumed by hatred for her child's father that she was totally blocked from perceiving in her son elements of goodness and charm which, of course, were there, as in the case of any child. As a result she was even lacking in full *agapē* for him. She saw to it that all physical and environmental needs were met, but she did not contrive even a counterfeit appearance of affection or response to the boy as boy. It is likely that she can't. She is sick, and her sickness is making him sick—to death. A positive step is needed; she requires psychiatric help. To procure it is her ethical duty, if she is capable of bringing herself to it; and it is the ethical duty of those close enough to her to have any influence on her, to seek to make this possible remedy available. As fast as she can be unblocked, the natural capacity of a mother to respond in love to that which is really lovable in a little boy will gain in strength and so will he.

case 54. Phony love, reorganized

Flora's block, in CASE 51, does not arise out of reaction to some third person; it is the direct result of how her mother is. Daily, presumably often hourly, contact is not remedying the situation; it is exacerbating it. What is needed is a fresh look, a new program. The aim, a change in her mother, the evocation of more of the good that is latent in her. Flora felt that living with her mother was the most "dutiful" alternative, deceived by the common assumption that that which is the most sacrificial is the most noble. She should try to find a senior citizens' home nearby. Here, exposed to day-by-day companionship with members of her peer group, most of whom would not feel particularly obligated to respond to anything other than attractive behavior, the mother might well bring to the fore whatever in her can afford a basis for mutual relationship, aided by natural, unpremeditated response to new faces and new personalities—people with similar interests, problems, memories and nostalgias—and grounds of complaint! At the same time, freed from an intolerable burden of time and tension, Flora can set her mind to planning special events and surprises to brighten her mother's weeks. And these might well produce in her mother warmth and charm to which Flora can genuinely respond. It can be presumed that her mother would resist the proposal that she live in a home for older persons, and that in the very discussion of it her register of self-pity and anxiety would rise markedly. But Flora's firmness in presenting this as the only alternative, though labeled by her mother as cruelty and coldness, would probably be vindicated by the outcome.

case 55. A "no-good whore," reappraised

As with any case, Mr. Driver's totally negative reaction to the prostitute (in CASE 52) involves subjective as well as objective factors. Maybe he should transfer the case to a colleague. But let's assume that this is unfeasible or that he is a sole functionary. There are two things which might achieve genuine response to the offender as person—one immediate and one longer range. In conversation he could deliberately seek out in her every expression and self-revelation even the smallest traces of goodness and basic niceness, such as her shy response to the everyday courtesies he has extended to her and the heretofore unnoticed warmth in talking about her family. At the same time he can leave himself open to unconditioned response, verbalized or not, whether momentary or geared only to a particular merit in her at the time. Two things will be happening: it will show through in his manner and bring immediate support to her sense of self-significance, and it will be bringing growth and heightened sensitivity to him—not only to his own benefit, but to the benefit of other probationers. Further, Mr. Driver can anticipate this in the preliminary period, and as time goes on, since he will now be consciously in a mood of looking for good reality to which to respond, there will be more there to which he can actually respond. A few sessions of night school and one day she says "isn't," not "ain't." On a better diet, she perhaps gains a little weight, not too ill-distributed. In her new job as gift-wrapper, she has concluded that a different cosmetic decor goes better. Once open, his observation automatically translates into manifest approval. He is beyond *agapē*. To her health and his.

Books and sermons on ethics and love put much stress on *agapē*, the source of its inspiration, the contexts of its activization, and the mode of its cultivation. *Erōs* is recognized as a fact, but rarely is anything found urging that there be more of it or explaining how to make it arise and grow. *Agapē* is seen as the result of conscious decision; *erōs* is viewed as an example of "the spirit bloweth where it listeth."

This is a half truth, in both the negative and the positive sense. *Agapē* is cool; *eros* is warm. *Agapē* can be unfeeling; comprehended in the definition of *erōs* is emotion. The action of *agapē* can be produced instantaneously by conscious decision. The emotion of *erōs* cannot similarly be effected. To parents who don't understand why their son doesn't go for a girl they feel is highly suitable for him, an unanswerable answer is, "She just doesn't turn me on." It's either there, or it isn't. This is illustrated in CASES 50, 51, and 52 in their original versions. *Agapē* was there in varying degrees; *erōs* wasn't.

But as the continuation of each illustration (CASES 53, 54, and 55) shows, neither do things have to be left *in statu quo* nor does one just have to wait for the spirit to blow as it listeth. The conscious will can play a part here just as it does in the case of *agapē*. While one cannot will, and thereby automatically effect, *erōs* (as one can *agapē*), one can change the context from a situation unfavorable to the appearing of *erōs* to one more favorable. Certainly one can better dispose oneself toward the appreciation of what may be attractive in another person. This can be done, depending on the situation, by getting rid of the barriers that blind one to the good qualities of another through greater understanding of oneself or the other, or by focusing attention more closely on the other's looks, conversation, and action. In short, more openness, more alertness, or both.

With everything done that a person can do, then *erōs* comes or it doesn't. But the oftener it does come to a person, the greater becomes his sensitivity to people and what they really are or can be. Further, the more loving one is becoming, the more lovable one becomes also. In a given relationship *agapē* can be a static position; *erōs* is dynamic. Love, *erōs*, begets love, and the love thus begotten increases the love of the initial giver. There are no pre-set limits to where this mutual circle of cause and effect can go. Great good can come—and also great complexity. To the acceptance of the one and the handling of the other we now turn.

chapter 10

HEALING WITH *ERŌS*

case 56. Institutions vs. persons?

Dianne Faber, an attractive young American girl, was finishing her fourth year as a student in Belfast, Ireland, preparing herself to be a religious social worker. She was filled with joy and eagerness on an afternoon in late spring, as she carefully dressed for her very important appointment with the Very Reverend John Moriarity, Superintendent of the District of Belfast, in whose jurisdiction she resided. In another month she would receive her degree and a few weeks later would marry Richard Kelley, whose ordination to the ministry would shortly follow. She felt happy and secure in her love for Richard and delighted at their plans for an exciting and important ministry in the slums of a large city, where together they could give their talents and love to the underprivileged. Richard was to take her to meet his superior because, in the first place, he was required to inform the prelate of his forthcoming marriage and, in the second place, he was proud of her and wanted the two to meet. When they arrived at Dr. Moriarity's office she was somewhat surprised at the lack of warmth and the air of solemnity with which the Superintendent greeted her.

The reason soon became obvious. After a brief greeting Dr. Moriarity seemed to gather his courage and plunged immediately to the heart of what he had to say. "Miss Faber, the records indicate that you have been married before and are a divorced woman, and therefore I cannot grant my permission for this marriage. If you persist in going through with it, then I will have to refuse to ordain Richard." Dianne was stunned, but she tried to explain that when she was seventeen she had indeed been married for a few weeks, quickly divorced, and the whole matter taken up with Dr. Moriarity's American counterpart in the same world church, the Very Reverend Thomas West, of Eastern California, who had told her that in the eyes of the Church her marriage had not existed and had granted her an annulment. Dr. Moriarity said that all of this was in the files and that he had thought it over but that there was nothing he could do about it. It was either career in the Church and no marriage, or marriage and no career in the Church. The choice was theirs.

After a couple of months of agonized thought, prayer, and discussion, Richard and Dianne were at an impasse. Their love was good, their desire to serve the Church real, and the sacrifice of one or the other seemed cruel and artificial, and beneficial to no one. Finally, they decided to leave the country they loved and move to Eastern California, where the annulment had been granted, and where they felt certain they could be accepted as persons having a great deal to contribute to the Church and to society. When they reached California, they were shocked when the Most Reverend Thomas West informed them that he would like very much to marry them and conduct Richard's ordination, but that he felt he must side with Dr. Moriarity in the matter because professional loyalty required mutual respect of his counterpart's decisions.

At the point where they were ready to turn their backs on the Church because of their acute disappointment and enlist in the Peace Corps, they met the Very Reverend Mark Huntington at a clergy conference in Eastern California. Still unmarried, still unordained, and still unemployed, they decided to discuss their problem one more time. After carefully and sympathetically listening, Dr. Huntington made an appointment with them on the last day of the clergy conference, and in the meantime investigated the facts.

When they met for their second talk, Dr. Huntington said, "We each look at these things in our own way, but my feeling is that your love has survived many disappointments and reversals, you will come into a marriage with maturity; your talents and love of the Church fit you for constructive work in the ministry, and if you wish to come to Southern Michigan we have a large city where your talents in urban ministry can be utilized. I am convinced of your sincerity, and if you can come with no bitterness in your hearts toward the other churchmen, I will be proud to have you as part of my team."

Did Dr. Moriarity, in hewing to the absolute "letter of the law" of his institution, benefit that institution?

Did Dr. West, in adhering to the "spirit" of the institution (backing up the decision of a fellow officer) benefit that institution?

Although the law was not in question, did Dr. Huntington, in choosing the young couple over the spirit of the institution harm the institution?

case 57. Darkest before the dawn

Married when they were quite young, Becky and Arnold had spent twenty years, sometimes with good will and sometimes not, trying to achieve at least a tolerable relationship. However, as the years went on, their estrangement became greater until finally they had not only lost any love or respect they might have had for each other, but the abrasiveness of their daily contacts was beginning to cause an active dislike and hatred to show through their words and actions, even when they tried to conceal it. Upon occassion they had consulted a marriage counselor and their pastor, but had gotten nowhere and now were reduced to shouting their story to their friends, acquaintances, each other, and their children. The real and the fancied sources of outrage in each were blurred to the point where their relationships with other people and even the basic goodness of each one was deteriorating. Their children, unhappy, confused, and intensely worried, were beginning to show signs of antisocial behavior. For reasons both religious and cultural ("divorce is always a bad thing and means that one or the other of them is really no good"), they had not sought the relief of divorce.

At a neighborhood meeting Becky met Charles. Throughout the course of their year-long affair Charles gave her an image of what a peaceful life with another man could be. He treated her with courtesy, listened to her problems, but at the end of the year they concluded they were not for each other.

Becky again turned to her marriage with Arnold with a kind of desperate eagerness, trying to make this existing relationship work, and found instead the old dissatisfactions and unhappiness more obvious than ever. She found herself longing, although not specifically for Charles, at least for the resurgence of confidence in herself as an attractive person that he had given her. Becky concluded that divorce was the solution to their misery; but Arnold's response was that he could use Becky's infidelity as grounds. His attorney convinced him that the public branding of their mother as an adulteress would only hurt the children. So Arnold permitted Becky to get the divorce on the grounds of mental cruelty, with an amicable settlement as to support and visitation rights of the parents with the children. Who broke up the marriage? Was the small-town community correct in whispering "same old triangle stuff"? Who displayed the greater *erōs* to whom?

case 58. Dawn breaks

The months following the granting of the decree proved to be the most bitter of all, with each person tending to blame the other and enduring spasms of guilt and feelings of failure. These were masqueraded as a demand for more child-support money by Becky, and cries of protest from Arnold that he couldn't afford what he was paying. Just as a period of grief and bereavement follows the death of a person, so a period of grief and bereavement followed the death of this marriage. The children continued to be torn.

Gradually the bitterness began to fade, and each person sought new interests and new friends. Having had the experience, even though briefly and furtively, of the genuine admiration and love of Charles, Becky was more receptive to new contacts, and in her work met Andy, a widower, with whom she shared mutual interests. Meeting became recognition; recognition became commitment. The first few months after their marriage were stormy ones for the children in terms of adjustment, but the youngsters began to respond to the serenity and accepting love in their new home and their antisocial behavior ebbed.

Arnold's more complex bitterness, ostensibly (conveniently?) intensified by Becky's involvement with Charles, was slower to abate. It wasn't until he had been going with

Amy, a woman whose love was matched by her patience, that he was able to look back at his first marriage and honestly recognize his part in its failure, as well as to understand its inherent wrongness. When this day of maturity was reached, he and Amy decided to marry and a fresh approach for life began for Arnold. The children, who frequently visited their father's home, were at long last relieved of the burden of their parents' unhappiness, and could turn all their energies, conscious and unconscious, to their own development.

The healing process in these heretofore unhappy people was completed when one day at a large gathering Arnold and Amy met Becky and Andy; and Arnold turned to his former wife, took her hand in his, and said simply and spontaneously, "I have never seen you look more beautiful."

case 59. Transference → countertransference

Carol Fisher came to Dr. Dwane Eliott, a psychological counselor, for help in overcoming the feelings of rage and rejection which she was experiencing following the end of what had been to her a deep and committed love affair with Brian, a successful married doctor in the community. She poured out the words to Dr. Eliott, and it became apparent that both she and her lover had believed that his marriage had been a bad one. When Brian gently informed her that he had decided to try again to make his marriage successful because of his three young children and for the sake of his good reputation in the community, Carol's fury knew no bounds because she thought, rightly or wrongly, that Brian had rewritten his marital history as a rationalization to cover what he must have felt as a guilty love for her. Dr.

Eliott listened patiently and was soon able to point out objectively to Carol that, whichever theory was correct, the doctor's wife in fact had priority. This calmed Carol's sense of outrage and focused her feelings properly on her grief at having lost Brian, and thus she felt helped immediately by Dr. Eliott's understanding.

As the weeks progressed and the outer layers of bitterness and resentment were removed, Carol emerged more and more as a bereft and lonely girl, whose confidence in her basic attractiveness had been badly shattered. Dr. Eliott, on the other hand, saw a different Carol, a pretty, sensitive, and winsome young woman, whose eyes sparkled with appreciation each time he complimented her on a new insight, and he found himself looking forward eagerly to her visits. Once Carol's great burden of self-revelation was delivered, she began to look with new eyes at Dr. Eliott, seeing a wise, kind and very attractive older man, and began to make excuses (quite delightfully transparent to him) for extra visits to his office.

One day Dr. Eliott did a most unusual thing. Quite without meaning to, he blurted out his hurt and disappointment at the reception by some colleagues of his of what he had considered to be a well-thought-out contribution to their particular discipline. Carol reached over and took his hand and they sat for a moment, giving strength one to the other. Some weeks later Carol came to Dr. Eliott's office, excitement shining in her face, and without preliminaries burst forth with the good news that she had met a man she wanted to marry. When he said, "I'd certainly like to meet him," she quickly said, "He's right out in the car." She ran to get him, and the rest of the hour was spent by the three in discussing with joy the coming marriage.

"Black is black and white is white" is a phrase as inapplicable to CASE 56, *Institutions vs. persons?* as it is to life in general. (If one asks a physicist, it is not even pertinent to optics.) We certainly can't get away with the oversimplification that Suprintendent Moriarity was a "bad guy" and Dr. Huntington a "good guy." Dr. Moriarity was charged with the good order of that part of the Church under his direct supervision, and part of that good order included the enforcement of the laws of the institution, one of which forbade the remarriage of divorced persons. We cannot even out of hand completely condemn Dr. West because of his professional loyalty, a valued and generally valuable precept among members of all professions. To be utterly fair and objective it must be recognized that institutions are made up of people. We might even consider the little combination of Richard and Dianne as a small "institution." Therefore, before we dismiss this case as simply institution vs. persons, we must be entirely clear in our thinking and not oversimplistic, thus leaping, for sentimental reasons, to what well may be a right answer.

Here is a true dilemma, to which Code ethics supplies an answer all right, but certainly a bleak and unloving one. The antinomist would be hard pressed for an answer and might sag, one fears, into a kind of "marshmallowy" indecisiveness from which he could not extricate himself long enough really to define the question. Here, for the sake of the institution and the persons involved we, more sharply than ever, must rely on situation ethics; and even situation ethics, resting upon responsibility alone, can't furnish the solution. Careful, wise, and responsible weighing leaves all the persons involved still looking for a guideline, which is not in evidence in the situation itself. This guideline has been spelled out in Chapter 7, and for shorthand style can be called the Greater Claim.

Could not Dr. Moriarity, who was well acquainted with the practices of his brother superiors, have simply sent the couple back to the United States where a less rigid law prevailed? Could not Dr. West have expressed his professional loyalty by an honest and thoughtful letter to Dr. Moriarity? The greater claim of love here demanded a little imagination which could be subsumed under the "whole mind" phrase of the *Sh'ma Yisrael*—or effort, subsumed under the "whole strength" phrase.

Each of the superiors presents a good case for *agapē*. All three had *agapē* for the institution, in theory. However, Dr. Huntington, with his *erōs* for the couple, in fact implemented the *agapē* for the benefit of the institution. This is not to say that *erōs* is always wise policy; it is only to be taken as a small indication that love is consistent with truth and need not always result in great dramatic decisions, although occasionally *erōs* seems to demand just that.

Having some intimation in the previous chapter that *erōs* can be evoked as well as arise spontaneously, we may find it worthwhile to question the possibility or even desirability of exercising control over it.

In CASE 57, *Darkest before the dawn,* the extramarital love of Becky and Charles might have given the unhappy woman an excuse mentally to rewrite her marital history and decide that her miserable marriage was actually dead, not just desperately sick. Instead she showed sufficient honesty and courage to try again to make it work. When it didn't, she could face this fact with as much bravery as possible and take the forthright action of asking for a divorce. From the vantage point of knowing the denouement of CASE 58, *Dawn breaks,* we see that this courageous facing up to the reality of the moribund marriage resulted years later, when she met her former husband at the party, in the ultimate moment of healing where genuine *erōs* could again flow between two people who easily could have gone to their graves still bitter and diminished as persons from their prior relationship.

If Becky had been a code ethicist she might have clung to her marriage on the widely held assumption that marriage is indissoluble. Or if her particular code were less rigid and more realistic in dealing with marital catastrophes it is hardly a gamble to assume that it would have forbade her adulterous relationship with Charles. But this was the very encounter that freed her and the others in her life sufficiently to begin the painful process of honestly examining the actual condition of the marriage. One cannot escape the totality of the one Claim in which truth and courage are the channels for receiving and expressing *erōs*. Here, one is struck by the feeling that Code ethicists have wrested aspects of the Claim out of the context of life and then clung with ferocity to these isolated tenets in spite of the dynamics of any given situation.

What possible room was left for *erōs* to be operative in the framework of Becky and Arnold's marriage? The wreckage was piling up to the point where even the innocent children were being stunted in their emotional growth. Insistence on its continuation on any ground would be an absolute affront to the Greater Claim. In retrospect, Arnold might even come to feel *erōs* for Charles although such sensitivity and imagination did not seem inherent in Arnold's personality. In this Case *erōs* required much courage and honesty, in contrast with just the minimum effort involved in CASE 56, *Institutions vs. persons?*

What then about CASE 59, *Transference→countertransference?* Here, love arose with no evoking. To accept this as a graceful and gentle vignette with no responsibility attached would be just as unrealistic as to insist that Becky and Arnold grimly "hang on." Perhaps, in the very long run, patience and understanding would have achieved roughly the same therapeutic end for the insecure, rejected Carol. The success or nonsuccess of any psychiatric or psychological technique is not at issue here. The fact is that Carol and Dr. Eliott were mutually attracted and that *erōs* with a sexual undertone was in operation. It is safe to assume that the skilled counselor recognized this if his more naïve counselee did not. Allowing it to develop mutually to a certain point, where healing was at its maximum and potential hurt at its minimum, produced an experience of grace for both of them.

How does *erōs* work? It operates in an ever widening spiral with truth and courage—honesty about oneself and one's situation, courage in evoking, applying, and controlling love, which in turn frees one for greater honesty, greater courage, and greater love. It requires every iota of talent and imagination inherent in a person. It is work, but it works!

chapter 11

DELIBERATION AND SPONTANEITY

case 60. Action against the odds

Four men were on a motor launch in shark-infested waters off a South Sea island. In a rough squall, Joe was washed overboard. Walt stripped down preparing immediately to jump in to try to save Joe. Jim and Milt struggled to restrain him. They had no less affection for Joe, but a quick exchange of words expressed their rapid but sincerely weighed decision that the odds were more than 50 per cent that, with the fury of the waves and the danger of the sharks, neither Joe nor his well-meaning lifesaver would emerge alive. But Walt felt there was a chance, tore himself free from his more prudent companions, and jumped in (even though he had a moment of guilty recollection of his wife and four small children—and his inadequate insurance). He had a difficult time of it; but the sea was not too much for his strength, not a shark appeared, and he was able to tow the nearly unconscious Joe back to the launch where they were pulled up the side to safety. Which was the more moral decision, Walt's or that of Jim and Milt?

case 61. Think or act?

In CASE 2, *"We're not hurting anyone,"* concerned with the affair of Bill and Dorothy, his office co-worker, there was time to think and talk about the rightness of the decision to go to bed the night they worked late and stayed in a downtown hotel. They were enjoying each other's company particularly that evening (they always had, but not with such keen awareness), and their rather unrestrained drinking in his hotel room afterwards did not encourage conscientious or probably even totally conscious weighing of plus and minus factors. Assuming for the purposes of the present consideration that it was wrong to proceed and thus launch what is now an ongoing affair, not intended to be such at the time, at what point in the relationship would one locate responsibility for reflection on the pros and cons?

case 62. Intuition—and grace

Frank, a state Attorney General running for reelection, was attending a state party convention. In accord with a deeply held conviction, his main object was to sell a resolution in favor of fair housing legislation, even though this objective was threatening his political future in the light of the growing white backlash in the state. He had hardly arrived in the convention city when he found that some of the supporters he had lined up were trimming and joined a "moderate" group. That very evening they met with him and had sought to dissuade him from presenting his resolution "at this time." He called his wife and found that she had been "reached" and was also urging him to desist. He could not persuade her to disclose who had talked to her ("that would be a breach of confidence"), reminding him vividly of her similar lack of supportiveness on other occasions in a marriage which for some time had been one in name only.

He worked half the night with an aide preparing a strong press statement, and before the opening session they worked in the press room making ink corrections in the copies and stapling the sheets. An attractive young lady, who had come from a distant part of the state to attend the convention, saw the need for help and, caring about the cause, pitched in. Preoccupied with the matter and the need of being on the floor for the first business of the convention, Frank reacted only subliminally; in fact as he rushed off he thanked her rather perfunctorily. As he argued for getting the matter on the agenda (his motion barely passed), he noticed her in the audience and felt somewhat sustained by her obviously approving expression.

That night as he was undressing for a much-needed night's rest, he learned by phone that, even as he was talking, right in the hotel a group was meeting to develop a smear against him, based on misleading data procured by the lobbyist for the state real estate association, to be brought to the floor before his fair housing resolution would come on. He spent the next two hours on the phone getting together data to use in his defense against the proposed resolution of censure, and in organizing his strategy. The next morning he shared the problem with a few old friends and colleagues and sensed differing responses: on the part of some, "That shows it wasn't smart to push something so radical"; on the part of others, diffidence of the "Well, that's politics" variety; on the part of still others, a certain real sympathy with no sign of wanting to get involved. When the matter came up later that day, the innuendos were articulated with no chance for Frank to state the facts that provided a conclusive answer, since right after the speeches of the proposer and seconder of the motion of censure a nondebatable motion to table was proposed and passed. Press, radio, and TV interviews multiplied and Frank tried to respond to all these requests both to try to clear his name and to develop public support for his upcoming resolution. In the few minutes he had that day to glance at his mail, he read hastily a note marked "personal":

You may not recall me; I know all that you're going through. The strain and underlying sadness show on your face. I came to this convention because I'm running; I was nearly falling apart when I left home. Seeing your courage has been helping hold me together. I think we could help each other just visiting a little while. If you can find the time, I'll be glad.

With respect,

LYNNE WILLIAMS

P.S. Call Room 432 or leave a message. I'll meet you any time, anywhere. L.

He didn't recall her but he was touched. He quickly forgot the message as he picked up the phone to hear the Governor, whom he had been representing as well as himself in the open occupancy fight, asking him to "cool it."

That evening as he was going down in the elevator Lynne got on at the fourth floor and said, without introduction, "You didn't let me hear from you; you know, my note." Still not quite putting it together, he played an old record: "I'm sorry; I've been pressed and so much paper has piled up; I'll get to it; thanks for writing me." The first floor reached, he darted off to join the Lieutenant Governor in the coffee shop. (The latter was fence-mending.)

He was pretty sleepless that night. He felt very alone. His

wife: she could have called. The mass media had carried everything; his perilous position was obvious. His "liberal friends": they seemed decimated. His time: how to make tomorrow count—the last day for corridor work and smoke-filled rooms before the big debate.

Exhausted even before he started the crucial day, he gave it all he had, right through until the evening. Now sleep! As he approached the elevator to go up, Lynne was there. Speaking directly, she said, "I've had no word from you." The record began playing again, "I'm sorry, I've been so pressed; and so much paper——" She interrupted and, calmly looking him straight in the eye, said, "*I'm* Lynne and *you're* Frank." He took her hand, went right into an open elevator, and without a word they went to his room. They embraced warmly; then—still without words—quickly undressed and went to bed. An hour later, over cigarettes, they talked a little. He didn't have to use many words to tell about all the pressures on him. She knew. Nor how down he had been feeling. She knew. But he encouraged her to open up. Her problem at home was difficult; but neither of them quite realized (his particular background in law practice had given him little experience as a counselor, directive or nondirective) as she poured it all out that she was also sorting it out. Then glancing at her watch, she said "It's eleven fifteen; you're going to sleep; tomorrow's important for you and for lots of people." He took her in his arms. They made love again, but more briefly, and then slept soundly until eight (his first good sleep for days). He hastily dressed, due at a breakfast meeting, saying to her, "You stay here, Lynne," (and he paused as he said her name—the last time it had been uttered was just before they took the elevator upstairs the night before), "—and take your time. I'll be back after this meeting and before I have to be on the convention floor."

He felt new confidence and courage as he joined the committee breakfast—though nothing was said by anybody that gave ground for it. Then back to his room. No Lynne. He noticed immediately that his papers were in order, in piles marked "Urgent," "Reroute," "Fan mail," "Negative fan mail," "Discard." And conspicuous, apart from all the rest, a note:

Frank, dear:
When you read this I'll be at the airport about to board a plane home. I think I can put my marriage together now; I feel like a woman again. You looked fine this morning. I'm so glad. I don't quite grasp what happened; I didn't plan for it to be that way—and I know you didn't (you had been downright neglectful!), but that's the way it was, and it was good. Forgive me for leaving just now. But I'm sure, all 'round, I should.

Love,
LYNNE

All that has been said before in this book presumed not only a conscious decision-making process but took for granted the existence of a span of time for conscious deliberation. But it's not always that way. When there's not time to think we tend to excuse people, including ourselves, for what we would otherwise judge to be malfeasance or nonfeasance. When there is time and when one has every reason to anticipate a time of called-for action or inaction, obviously there is a positive responsibility to face the matter, to reflect on it early enough in the game to implement the decision at the critical time.

The application to CASE 61, *Think or act?*, is pretty clear. An emotional feeling was asserting itself during the evening of genuine work. The post-work possibilities—"Thanks so much. Good night." "Why not come to my room for a night cap?"—were worthy of pondering. *If* the best answer to the ultimate question would be No (and we're assuming that to be the case for the purpose here) then the best answer to the threshold question would be to plan to utter the first, not the second, of the remarks. And on Dorothy's part, to plan to answer the second set of words—the possibility of his saying them not being remote! —with "I'd love to, but I'm bushed and I'll take a cab home." Or if one or both felt secure about restraint later, then a determination to limit consumption and show of affection would be relevant, then "Good night"—spent separately.

But in CASE 60, *Action against the odds,* Walt, Jim and Milt cannot necessarily be held responsible for thinking out in advance whether (*if* there were to be a squall and *if* one of the others were to be washed off) to jump in or not, calculating the chances of survival, the weight of family and other responsibilities, the amount of insurance, and the rest. What to do when it happens? The answer would be intuitive, not reflective. But if the decision is not compulsive and depends less on weighing the moment than on a past experience in making decisions, then the decision can be seen as showing the style of life of each man. As it turned out, Walt looks like the finer man; if it had turned out differently, he would have been adjudged a well-meaning fool and the others wise men. Nor can we judge them as cowardly just because Walt's impetuous step was successful. The old saw about hindsight and foresight is applicable. Anyway, some of the factors that could make the difference between tragedy and success were beyond the control of any of the men. Ethics and ethical choice don't really enter here except for legitimate admiration for Walt's impulse and courage—rendered after the event.

So, via CASE 62, *Intuition and grace,* we come to the

question: Can there be a positive ethical quality to an intuitive, unreflective decision—calling for no courage to act, but where cogitation and dialogue about pros and cons would be inconsistent with the happening itself—where the unexpected moment seems to be charged with grace?

When deep need is sensed, a full response carries its own instructions. As to ethics it requires no unusual effort for events swiftly to take their course. To have blocked the outcome or to have turned it into a calculated decision could well be adjudged as unethical. Granted that such moments are not common, it can be wrong to miss the few which present themselves. Even in this case we cannot give an absolute answer, and could not even with fuller facts. But only the most thoroughgoing Code ethicist would presume confidently to pronounce a negative judgment. To love and to be loved, to want and know one is wanted—and precisely at the right time—is not the most common thing in the world. There are times for spontaneous action, as well as times for lengthy deliberation.

These Cases, especially the first and third, underline the difficulty of making ethical judgments about people in complex situations (and most situations are more complex than the cases here described). Not only are ethical considerations involved in such assessments; the very matter of making judgments at all involves ethical considerations. To this matter we now turn.

chapter 12

WHO'S TO JUDGE—AND WHAT?

case 63. Who gets the job?

The Vestry of St. Vitus-in-the-Vale had reduced its list of candidates for election as Rector to Dr. Wilburn and Father Smythe. Most of the vestrymen were very impressed by each. At a time in the parish history when through an overly ambitious building program their financial picture was shaky, they quite reasonably gave attention, among other things, to the record of each man in his present and previous cures in regard to the development of each man's budgetary program. Here they discovered contrasting pictures. In places quite comparable in situation, Dr. Wilburn had left each church in a real financial hole—in fact one place had to close soon after he left. Father Smythe had left the churches he had served in sound condition, in two instances with all mortgages paid off.

More sensitive than most vestrymen, they checked to see if any differentiating factors had obtained, such as the average income level of the respective parishioners, the strength and imagination of the stewardship programs, and the general level of pledges to each church. After making careful inquiries they found that each man had served in very similar churches where in each case over one half the church's income was provided by four or five very wealthy members.

More than these simple financial facts was learned through conversations with various members of the parishes where each candidate was now serving. While the Senior Warden of Father Smythe's present parish discussed the budgetary picture with the "investigators," he took them for a tour of the church plant and proudly pointed out two new and expensive stained glass windows donated during Father Smythe's tenure, some beautiful Italian marble sculpture, and handsome new altar furnishings. He also told them of the peaceful place of refuge the rector had created and for which many of the older members of the congregation were particularly grateful. He did comment rather ruefully that not as many young persons seemed to attend the church these days.

It was easy for members of the committee to check on Dr. Wilburn's church because it was in an adjoining neighborhood of the same large city and the make-up of the congregation was almost identical. There they talked with the Junior Warden because when they called upon the Senior Warden for information about Dr. Wilburn they were met first with a rather tight-lipped silence followed by the remark, "Perhaps things will be better if he goes; but Christian charity would prevent my telling you what I really think of Dr. Wilburn." The Junior Warden, a Negro, spoke of his Rector with enthusiasm and joy and said that because of his unceasing championship of the civil rights of the minority members of the congregation, there had been a number of transfers into other parishes and a few big pledge cuts. A discussion with the Treasurer of the parish, who was generally supportive of his pastor, revealed that the Vestry had already reached its maximum borrowing limit from the bank in its earnest effort to pay current bills.

Whatever effect, either way, the degree of social activism or quietism displayed by each candidate might have on the determination, it is obvious that in the present circumstances of St. Vitus-in-the-Vale, important in the discussion and the election of the next rector will be the facts having to do with the fund-raising potential of Dr. Wilburn and Father Smythe. As to this question, which is at the fore, and as to the other questions which are implied in this brief outline, what precisely is the nature of the judging? Properly, are the vestrymen, on a basis of the available data, only judging past performance with an eye to likely future performance? Or are they judging *men*?

case 64. "Publicity-mad"

Alfred Lawrence, an attorney, had occasion to serve as counsel for the defendant in three cases involving arrest and prosecution of male homosexuals. In one case, he was convinced that the accused was innocent but had been framed by agents of an opposing political candidate; in another, he had every reason to believe that his client thought he was a victim of police blackmail; in the third, the client admitted to him that he and an adult friend, both single, had discreetly been sexually involved for some years. As a result of these professional assessments and after careful thought and study on the subject, Lawrence reached the conclusion that there should be no criminal sanctions against freely consenting adult homosexual behavior.

A good speaker, Lawrence frequently gave talks before various church and community groups. He now began to speak on this topic, seeking to develop public opinion in favor of amendment of the Penal Code of his state. In due time he successfully introduced a resolution before the state Bar Convention authorizing a study commission on the subject, and he was appointed chairman. He gave a good deal of his time to the work and was increasingly asked to speak to larger and larger groups. At the same time there was more and more press coverage of his remarks, and he often appeared on radio and TV discussions.

The appearances on TV occurred for a number of reasons: Occasionally he related to the press factual summaries or interim reports adopted by his committee. The group sponsoring an address sometimes informed the press of the forthcoming occasion and included excerpts of his scheduled address. But, more generally and increasingly, the mass media on their own initiative covered almost any appearance he made.

There was considerable opposition to his views within the state Bar Association as well as outside. This opposition was verbalized on the merits, and there was also growing articulation of a personal "put-down" in private conversations, in some public gatherings, official and unofficial. In two newspaper editorials there were statements such as: "Lawrence is after the publicity—it does something for his ego," "It's a case of self-advertisement," "He's just trying to build up his law practice," "Lawrence is publicity-mad." When he heard of such comments he flatly denied them. Was this the right response?

case 65. Protégé/gigolo

Alfred's wife, Betty Lawrence, intensely resentful at the amount of time Alfred's "campaign" was taking, began to join in the personal detraction. She became attracted to Jon Benton, a poor and improvident novelist-hopeful who was a friend of a friend, and she began to create opportunities to see him. Whether due to preoccupation with his writing or lack of interest in her, he made no moves, in spite of the growing opportunities becoming obvious, to enter into a liaison with her. Having means of her own, finally she offered to be his "angel" on a basis of five hundred dollars a month. Before long he was in her bed. She gained a reputation for being a patron of the arts and enjoyed hearing praise of her generosity. Was this acclaim justified? She believed it.

case 66. Was there "malice"?

When Don Mayfield was editor of the Clevetown *News-Transcript*, he consistently failed to promote Bill Sanders, a reporter of long experience with whose work he was not particularly impressed and whom he did not like. Don ran for office and was elected County Assessor; whereupon he severed his connection with the newspaper. A year later Bill wrote for the newspaper an exposé of Don's brief period of administration, asserting that he was corrupt in his assessment policies and had been advantaged by unjustified instances of leniency. Don, through counsel, demanded retraction. This being refused, he sued for libel, naming as defendants both the *News-Transcript* and Sanders. Though counsel for the latter was unable to support the defense of truth, they were able to rely on a recent decision of the

United States Supreme Court holding that defamation against a public figure was not actionable unless the plaintiff could prove malice. To this end, Don's attorneys introduced various items of testimony covering a period of years. The judge instructed the jury in accordance with the Supreme Court decision. Hence the jury in its deliberations focused its attention on this issue. In the course of its discussion one of the jurymen said, "We are not in a position to judge anyone's motives; in fact, in a recent sermon my minister said this was wrong." A fellow juryman retorted, "But that's precisely what the judge has told us we have to do, and we have to do it. And as I see it . . ." Which of the two was right?

Quite apart from the ethical question of whether we ought to judge others or to what degree, the advance of depth psychology has limited considerably the scope of our doing so successfully. We now realize more and more how complex such questions are. Even if we could get inside a person's mind and assess his conscious motivation (as distinguished from what he *says* his motive is), this process would not touch the factors in his *unconscious* mind. Arising from the unconscious in some cases are compulsions that eliminate freedom of choice in action; in other cases, freedom to act is somewhat curtailed or the decision on how to act is loaded by urges and drives from the unconscious mind. The formative sources of these compulsions and drives are highly diversified and complex in their history, and in most cases their existence, nature, and degree of force are unknown even to the actor, let alone to outsiders. Even a psychoanalyst, after hours of interviewing, can draw only tentative conclusions about the degree to which certain actions or patterns of action are the result of free decision based on consciously perceived aims and the degree to which they are grounded in unconscious forces. To the extent that unconscious forces are operative, almost inevitably the conscious mind supplies, automatically more often than not, a rationalization (or true assessment) supportive of a sense of integrity. The presence of this more observable layer, in some cases "cover," adds to the difficulty of discerning the true motivational picture.

So there is an empirical basis as well as a moral one behind the injunction attributed to Jesus, "Judge not . . ." and St. Paul's "I judge no man, not even myself." Quite personally and existentially did the latter recognize the fact of freedom-limiting compulsions. A free translation of St. Paul's passage in Romans would run, "There is another dimension in my make-up which wars with the norms of my conscious mind, and those things which I mean to do, I don't seem able to do and those things which I wouldn't do are the very things I find myself doing" (7:15-24). Thus actions are not easily interpretable as a free saying of yea or nay, with good motive and evil motive easily discernible. When it comes to judging a man, others don't really know "the inside story" all that well; the man himself doesn't.

So in CASE 64, *Publicity-mad,* others were simplistic in defining Alfred's motives. But at the same time, Alfred, though doubtless sincere, was naïve in flatly denying the charges. He could well have said, freely granting that he wanted publicity for his cause and for its supporting arguments, "I'm not conscious of seeking publicity for a build-up or to get ahead." But as to all that might be operative at the unconscious level he could honestly only say, "I don't really know"—the clear implication being that his accusers didn't either.

Conversely, in the case of his wife (CASE 65, *Protégé*

/gigolo) those attributing a noble motive to Betty could be right in whole or part, even though her generous support of the artist seems to have had to do with her achievement of a much desired personal outcome. Her attraction to him was at the least the catalyst for her financial decision; but that fact does not of itself foreclose the possibility that she really wanted to encourage creative writing.

Nor can we simplistically label Jon a gigolo. Quite apart from the morality of the relationship on other grounds, her step may have been the catalyst that caused him to pay attention to her as a person, and it is quite possible that his making love to her was at the start, or became, the expression of his loving *her*, not just her stipend. The opposite of these possibilities cannot be ruled out either—nor can the strong possibility of a mixture of motives. Refraining from judgment is the only proper response to the situation. But that Betty is at present being assessed affirmatively is a better thing than if she were beng judged negatively: assumption of innocence until guilt is proved is not just a legalism; it is a jurisprudential maxim grounded in good ethics and sound depth psychology.

Therefore no judgments at all? No, this would be an absolute, and like all absolutes, destructive of responsibility in certain contexts. The Vestry in CASE 63, *Who gets the job?* have to get off the ground: they have to choose a Rector. And this involves a judgment. But it is important to notice the limited scope of the judging. They are, or should be, trying to estimate the likely functioning of each of two priests in what for either one of them wuld be a new scene. And this they are trying to infer from objective data as to the past functioning of each. Hopefully, they are not presuming to judge either *man* or his motives.

What about situations where, on the other hand, a decision is called for and the motive of a man is the precise issue? In the light of the Supreme Court decision, sound or unsound, referred to in CASE 66, *Was there "malice"?* the sole question for the jury is malice/no malice. The law itself—"secular," but often more moral than the less careful judgmentalism of many Christians—recognizes that inner states of mind can rarely be established by proof. Hence, in virtually all areas of law, civil and criminal, a proper modesty as to likely knowledge is shown, and the determination is limited to the legality of actual behavior, something far more within the realm of probitive ground. But there are a few exceptions,[1] and in this Case we are dealing with one of them.

But even here the precedents based on centuries of judicial experience recognized that actual malice is very difficult to arrive at conclusively. What would almost be required is a verified statement of the defendant as to his evil intent—and even such a statement would not be necessarily true in all cases. Hence the category of *constructive malice.* In order to try to do adequate justice to the parties, the jury is allowed to draw a plausible inference simply from external behavior. But actually it is the latter (the *behavior*) which is the subject of the objective fact-determination.

The fact that Don Mayfield didn't promote Bill Sanders does not really prove that Sanders' story about him (accurate or inaccurate) arose out of a malicious intent toward his former superior. Nonpromoted employees have been known to be decent toward their bosses or ex-bosses. But if conclusive evidence had been introduced to establish that Sanders had made little investigation and had no real

[1] On the difficulties and anomalies involved in the determination of inner states of mind, see the author's "What Is Second Degree Murder in California?", *Southern California Law Review* 9 (1936).

facts to go on in what he wrote, then there is constructive malice. The latter concept is based in this regard on a nice (but perhaps overoptimistic) view of human nature which assumes that people will not, with good heart, make damaging charges about the behavior of others unless they have some factual basis for it. So the fact (i.e., Sanders' having no facts) added to this general assumption, constituting together constructive malice, added to the context of the past employer-employee relationships for background "color," could allow a jury to land on the side of "malice" rather than on the side of "no malice." Whether or not each juryman would in fact be all this precise in his mind on what his vote should represent, nevertheless this is properly what each should be concerned with. At most a juryman is judging behavior and its implications, not judging the man or his *actual* internal motives.

In our analysis the drawing of such fine lines is not being legalistic. Here sophistication is a form of charity—and of true honesty.

If such care is called for in situations at law where at various levels judgment is institutionally required, all the more should judgmentalism as to persons and motives be avoided on the part of volunteer "judges" whose often too peremptory conclusions are not required business or professional choices or judicial decisions, but rather gossip about someone—darts thrown at a selected human dartboard. Not only charity, not only honesty about what one really "knows," but also *true reverence*—"knowing one's place" in relation to God—call for working recognition of the affirmation that there is only One, to quote a medieval prayer, "unto whom all hearts are open, all desires known, and from whom no secrets are hid."

chapter 13

DECIDING FOR PERSONS

case 67. No accounting for tastes

Fred and Alistair were having a leisurely dinner at a fine French restaurant, which had an equally good American cuisine. While examining the menu during their third cocktail, Fred decided to have snails for a starter, and Alistair decided to have blue point oysters. Fred objected, "This is a *French* restaurant; you ought to have snails. Have you ever tried them?" Alistair shook his head. Fred pursued the point: "You at least ought to try them!" "I don't like the idea somehow," Alistair answered, "and anyway I'm very fond of oysters, especially blue points when they are available." Fred followed up, raising his voice, "I think it's unreasonable to be against something you've never tried!" "Drop it," Alistair retorted, "I'm having oysters." Was Alistair unfair?

case 68. Sticky fingers

Mary was a good maid, but things had been disappearing around the house. Mr. and Mrs. Williams, for whom she had worked for some years, became especially alert.

Before dinner one evening they marked two ten-dollar bills and left them on the sideboard in the dining room and then sat in the living room in a location which enabled them to see the sideboard via a large mirror which hung above it. Shortly thereafter they saw Mary glance at the bills, pick them up, and pocket them. After dinner, when she had gone to a room in which she customarily changed from her uniform to her street clothes, they quickly checked her purse and saw the marked bills. They left them in her purse for a number of reasons. They did not want to come to a showdown with Mary because they liked her work very much and didn't want to go to the trouble of breaking in someone new. Also they were aware of her grave financial plight during this period because she had considerably overextended herself in refurnishing her small apartment. The Williamses were also conscious of the fact that she was going through an emotional crisis over the break-up of her marriage. They figured it would be really the most helpful thing at the right time to let her know that they had noticed the petty thefts and to talk it over with her understandingly. But they did not feel that now was the time.

After this particular incident they did finally install locks on the liquor cabinet and on a drawer or two in the bedroom in which they were careful thereafter to keep any valuable jewelry. A day or two later a friend of Mrs. Williams dropped by in the late afternoon. Mrs. Williams was dressing for a party while she chatted with her friend and the latter noticed that Mrs. Williams unlocked the dresser drawer to get a necklace and a bracelet. Later, when Mrs. Williams offered a drink, her friend noticed that she similarly unlocked the liquor cabinet before fixing cocktails. "Why do you lock things up around here now?" the friend asked. Mrs. Williams told her why.

"I think the whole thing is unfair," the friend insisted. "I mean—to judge Mary—and a good girl she is—without confronting her with the charges, giving her a chance to answer." Mrs. Williams tried to explain that she and her husband still liked Mary, liked her work, and at this point didn't want to embarrass her and break the harmonious relationship with her. "In fact," she continued, "we understand her present situation and will try to handle it at the right time. Meanwhile we're not eager to have part of her problem solved at our expense—at least in that way." Were the Williamses being unfair to Mary?

case 69. Kangaroo court

Senator Stewart for some years had been the most vocal member of the State Senate Committee on Education. Increasingly over the years it seemed to many that he was going too far in bringing to light evidence on what he felt were widespread crippling defects in the educational philosophy and school practice in the State. These critics also felt that he was too avant-garde in avidly promoting the ideas of reform-minded professors of education in support of what conservative opinion regarded as a radical approach to pedagogy and to the whole style of educational communication. A number of his senatorial colleagues had warned him from time to time that he was going too far, that his statements were disturbing many "little people" in the State and undermining their confidence in the school system. Finally, considerable sentiment developed in the Senate that he should be unseated.

The achievement of this result in this particular State called for a complicated procedure: (a) the filing of charges by three Senators with a specified seniority in the Senate,

(b) action by an investigating committee required to be appointed by the Lieutenant Governor as chairman of the Senate, (c) indictment by a special grand jury appointed by the committee, consisting half of Assemblymen and half of other citizens of the State, (d) judgment by a senatorial court of nine members with staggered terms, (e) affirmation of the judgment by an appellate senatorial court similarly elected, and, finally, (f) confirmation of the judgment by a two-thirds vote of all the Senators.

A few weeks before the Legislature was due to convene (though, incidentally, the Legislature as such had legally nothing to do with the process at this point), a Senator Walters prepared a draft document of the type required to institute the proceedings and procured on it the signatures of a dozen Senators, about half from his region of the State, who had been rather stand-pattish on the enactment and implementation of reform legislation (on matters other than education) which had been consistently favored by the majority. Most of the others who added their signatures were leading members of the opposite party from that of Senator Stewart. Senator Walters then mailed the draft to the rest of the Senators, including junior members who were not qualified to sign on for the initiation of an unseating procedure but who would count as part of the final court of review, namely, the Senate itself. He sought the signatures, as co-presenters, of all the Senators—with the exception of one category: in his communication he recognized that those Senators on the trial and appellate courts could not properly sign on; nevertheless he invited them to affirm to him in writing their advance support of the proposed action. Attached to the draft statement was a collection of purported statements by the accused, some of which were accurate, some of which were literally correct but quoted out of context, and some of which were misquotations. An aide of the Senator had put this together. Because of a trip the Senator had to take before it was completed, he hadn't seen it, nor had some—perhaps any—of the original signators. As a result he picked up about fourteen additional signatures. He then wired other Senators to this effect: "If you don't sign on, how will you facc your conservative constituents?" But this brought few additions to the list.

A few days before the Legislature was to convene, the Lieutenant Governor, as presiding officer of the Senate, mailed a communication to the Senators. He indicated that he had tentatively selected a special committee to study the effects in the Senate and in the State of the actual starting and carrying through of the proposed action for unseating Senator Stewart. The Lieutenant Governor expressed himself as taking a dim view of the use of this method of getting at the issue, sensing the likelihood of divisiveness in the Senate and among the citizenry. He indicated that he would seek validation of a committee on the opening day of the session, and if supported in his approach, he would then announce the full roster of the other members of the committee, having named in the letter the proposed chairman, an elder statesman in the Senate.

On receipt of the Lieutenant Governor's letter, Senator Stewart promptly called the proposed chairman, a Senator Rockford, and asked for the opportunity to appear before the committee and be heard. His elder senatorial brother said quite frankly that it was unlikely that he would be allowed to appear, because what he had in mind to solve the problem wouldn't make Senator Stewart's appearance particularly appropriate. As the legislators gathered at the Capitol, the accused Senator approached the Lieutenant Governor and asked him to arrange with Senator Rockford that he be allowed to be heard. But he received only the assurance that the Lieutenant Governor would speak to the tentative chairman about it. The as yet unnamed special committee met Sunday afternoon before the opening of the Legislature the next day. That morning the committee was officially set up, and the Lieutenant Governor named the full committee of eight.

To the surprise of Senator Stewart and those sympathetic to his ongoing cause, three of the appointees were from the list of the original dozen accusers: the instigator and one who was a very loyal member of the opposite political party were included; included also was another accuser and two others who had been members of still another committee in the previous session of the Legislature. (This earlier committee in response to a petition of a group of predominantly radical-right Assemblymen, had agreed upon charges boldly impugning Senator Stewart's motives but had been persuaded at the last minute by some liberal members of the Senate that it would be impolitic—and probably unsuccessful—to bring forth their charges before the Senate, where a considerable vocal opposition could be guaranteed.) The committee now being officially set up (though it had already done its major work), Senator Stewart again asked Senator Rockford for a hearing and was tersely informed that the tentative committee had voted unanimously the day before that he not be allowed to appear or be heard. Senator Stewart was astounded, as were the increasing group of Senators who were rallying to his support.

A special order of business was set for the following afternoon for the hearing of the committee's report and action thereon. Stewart first heard when the whole Senate did, and learned to his astonishment that, while the committee recommended against an unseating procedure on the ground that such an action would look to the public like an attempt to repress free inquiry and rigidity on possible alternate views of public policy, including educational philosophy, they nevertheless proposed a censure in terms that would constitute judgments on his personal and official character. For example, the committee unanimously recommended that the Senate adjudge that Senator Stewart was "totally irresponsible," was "insensitive" to the devotion of the people of the State to the conventional ways of education, was guilty of "cheap vulgarization," and "crude characterization" of traditional principles of pedagogy. In fact they concluded that his "often obscure and contradictory" views weren't worth the trouble and pain of a trial, the Senators having more important things to get on with.

A special rule of order was adopted by the Senate, allowing only an hour's debate, with the last ten minutes to be left to the accused. About a third of the Senators vigorously opposed the censure resolution. First they tried to table it. Failing in that, they sought delay until the next day's session, in order to permit reflective thought and better preparation for debate. Turned down on that, they barely gained, after a parliamentary hassle, an additional hour for debate. They offered various modifying amendments, but succeeded in only one instance: the adverb "totally" was subtracted from the adjective "irresponsible." One of their number pointed out that the present proceeding was in fact a trial —without the hearing of evidence provided in the established trial procedures and with no adequate opportunity for the accused to be prepared, or to be allowed adequately, to defend himself and the cause which he represented (which had fairly widespread support throughout the State and in the Senate itself). The sentiment of a considerable segment of the Senate was expressed by one of the supporters of the resolution of censure when he said, with feeling, that the charges were unfair and unsupported, but that he would vote for it in the hope of avoiding a worse evil, namely, an unseating trial.

In the end the censure was passed by a two-thirds vote. This action was followed by three things: a minority position paper fully supportive of Senator Stewart's program, then a public dissociation, one by one, of various Senators from the action of the Senate, and, finally, the filing by Senator Stewart with the presiding officer, as permitted by a rule of the Senate never before put to use, of a document co-signed, as required, by two fellow Senators, demanding that the senatorial judicial route for unseating be followed. "The importance of my cause and the need of a charter of clear freedom for others vigorously to support it," he said to the Senate as he presented the paper to the Lieutenant Governor, "require that I take this step setting in motion what all of us had wanted to avoid. I will now through this painful procedure ahead (which *does* provide for appearance and hearing) be exonerated or unseated. At stake is no less than my honor as a man, my integrity as a Senator, and the importance of the cause of which I have become the focus. So I've put my seat in this Senate on the line." Some of his colleagues called him "stubborn," others "legalistic." Was he?

Seeking to provide for justice is part of what it means to love persons. Justice generally requires the sifting of data, the distinguishing of fact from rumor and opinion, and the reflective reaching of carefully framed conclusions on a basis of fact—and fact alone. Any person who has a legitimate interest at stake in any case or controversy is supposed to be allowed to participate in the process in an adequate way. The Fifth and Fourteenth Amendments to the federal Constitution call this adequate way *due process of law.* Those who provide for it for others or demand it for themselves are not being legalistic. In fact due process guarantees are not just a matter of law; underlying them is an important ethical principle. To give one an opportunity to hear the specific evidence to be adduced against him, to confront his accusers, to cross-examine them, and to introduce independent testimony on his own behalf is a recognition of his basic personhood. To deny it is to violate him as a person—whatever might be the soundness or unsoundness of any conclusions which, at the end of the process, are reached for or against him. Also experience has shown that this method, by and large, is a protection against unfair judgments. And it is almost too obvious to say that the latter hope has to do not with an abstraction but has to do with persons.

However, not all judgments affect other people—or at least their legitimate interests. In CASE 67, *No accounting for tastes,* Fred pressed Alistair to evaluate snails after actual testing of the datum of his response to eating them. Alistair was in no mood to cooperate. But his resistance was actually not unethical. First of all, it really wasn't any of Fred's business; and, second, it wasn't evident that by his nonparticipation in the experiment Alistair would be denying some need of his own health and well-being, thus violating an ethical obligation.

In the next Case (68, *Sticky fingers*), no deprivation was visited on the maid by the Williamses' reticence, for the time being, about confrontation on the petty theft. The facts were completely evident and quite properly served as a basis for precautions in the future. And when things became right for it in Mary's life, they were prepared to take the matter up with her for whatever help it might be to her. Meanwhile, life went on as usual for them and Mary. It was doubtless unethical for Mrs. Williams to tell her friend about it when quizzed about the locks, since the friend had no need to know this about Mary (as would undoubtedly be the case were she considering employing Mary, which she was not). But since the friend was in no position to disadvantage Mary, Mrs. Williams' reply to her friend's puzzlement about the locks was an understandable "venial sin" in the Department of Gossip.

Different in almost every respect is the third Case (69, *Kangaroo court*). It may well be that with provision of the requested appearance and hearing, ample time for preparation of the defense, and presentation of evidence (such as the thousands of letters to Senator Stewart from citizens who have *not* been put off by his comments, who have been disturbed by the educational status quo and offended by the methods of its supporters, and who are eager for the radical reforms for which the Senator was giving such a strong lead)—with all this there still might have been a recommendation of censure by the special committee and its adoption by the Senate. But he would have been treated as a person—as would the many people in the State for whose aspirations he had become a focus—not the least a third of his fellow Senators.

Apparent from this Case is another value of the dialogue which is due process: the possibility of reaching a *tertium quid,* a sound new approach not identical with the two initial positions. More specifically in this Case, the wording of the resolution of the Senate might have been modified—

not necessarily on a basis of political compromise but as a result of the careful examination of all the facts adduced and tested. In fact, the residuum might have been corporately agreed-upon conclusions, one or all of which Senator Stewart might have been the first to concur in—with honesty and good heart conceding that some of his points and ways of presenting them were not totally sound. Thus there could have come healing and greater wisdom all around. But the chance for that was lost by the denial of appearance, hearing, and presentation of facts at a time *before* the committee, on its own, had arrived at a mind-set. Instead, a lengthy adversary proceeding is ahead for the State, dividing Senator from Senator, citizen from citizen.

Thus we see that the *way of deciding* can be as important as *the decision.* As the author used to say every year as he opened his law school course in Procedure, with reference to the customary distinction between procedural and substantive law: procedure *is* substance.[1]

Legal and governmental structures, even the generally accepted forms of due process, are not absolutes; but we have just seen how, in given contexts, they can serve the protection and fulfillment of personhood. What about laws and customs that appear to block personal protection and fulfillment? To this type of conflict we now turn.

[1] "In society the given rules of law, including those of procedure, are part of the fabric of expectancies. So viewed, rules of procedure—not of jurisdiction, for that matter—really are *substantive,* not just 'adjective law.' They are intended to serve basic purposes: they are not merely technicalities or machinery." The author's *Beyond the Law,* Rosenthal Lectures, Northwestern University Law School (New York: Doubleday & Company, Inc., 1963), p. 41.

chapter 14

STRUCTURE AND CONSCIENCE

case 70. Red/green

Myrtle is a philosophically minded artist who has strong convictions not only that art should reflect life, but that life and its structures should be informed by an artistic perception. To her red is an action color, signifying movement, and green is a static color representing quiet and tranquillity. She finds quite contradictory to these intuitions the virtually universal provision of traffic laws that red requires a stop and green permits movement ahead. As she drives her automobile should she follow her deeply felt aesthetic principles or obey the law?

case 71. "Live-in"

The State fair-housing law had just been repealed by the Legislature. Promptly the Apartment Owners Association of Atlantic Heights adopted a policy which would call for each owner systematically to refuse to renew the leases of Negro families in the area. When the lease of the Andrewses, a Negro couple, came up for renewal, the manager of Equality Manor explained kindly to the couple that, while he liked them personally and while they had been fine tenants, the owner felt he must follow the agreed-upon policy of the Association—and that in fact he himself believed that the three vacancies in the apartment house resulted from the Andrewses' presence there. In accordance with a policy adopted as a counter measure by the new Negro Tenants League of Atlantic Heights, the Andrewses declared that they were staying put. Were they justified in refusing to move?

case 72. Civil disobedience from the right

The U.S. Securities and Exchange Commission has amended its regulations which require the registration, for the purpose of "full disclosure" of securities to be offered for sale, to include the offering to the public through interstate channels of part interests in commercial property developments. Atherton, Kent, and Widdifield, investment bankers who were all ready for the national promotion of several such schemes, sought advice of counsel. The latter rendered his opinion to the effect that the Commission's amended regulation is *ultra vires* (beyond the scope of the regulatory power given to the Commission by the Securities Act of 1933). Consultation with the Office of the General Counsel of the S.E.C. quickly made it evident that the Commission and its attorneys were of the distinctly opposite opinion and also that the repeal of the amendment by the Commission was out of the question. This information was followed by consultation among a number of financial firms, and there was mutual agreement that it was important that the legality of the regulation be tested and, as they hoped, be judicially rejected. In fact a number of interests and associations agreed to file briefs *amici curiae* when the test case reached appeal, if things should take this course.

Thus supported, and with their purpose clear, Atherton, Kent, and Widdifield, without registration of the proposal with the S.E.C., publicly offered the part interests for sale. Was it ethical thus flatly to disobey the regulation?

case 73. Secret nonconformity

In one of the States there has been a movement of several years' standing which is supported by various church and civic groups. It seeks to liberalize the State abortion law to permit abortion, at the request of the pregnant mother and with the consent of the given hospital's therapeutic abortion committee, in cases of rape, incest, and threatened malformation of the child, for example, from German measles contracted by the mother early in the pregnancy. To date, legislation introduced each year has failed to get out of committee, or has been tabled by the legislature itself.

An investigation under the auspices of the Attorney General and the State Board of Medical Examiners has brought to light that many physicians, with the consent of the Board involved, have been performing abortions under the circumstances mentioned, especially in cases of German measles. A score or more doctors were served with notices of hearing for the revocation of their licenses to practice. A bishop, who had figured rather prominently over the years in the efforts for legislative reform of the abortion law, declared through the mass media that these physicians were to be praised for their civil disobedience, putting the interests of their patients ahead of an archaic law for the amendment of which every effort had been made. Was he right in designating their actions as civil disobedience?

case 74. Civil disobedience/vigilantism

Civil rights organizations were convinced that the Fourth National Bank was practicing racial discrimination in hiring, contrary to the provisions of the State Fair Employment Practices Act. Representatives of these groups sought a conference with the manager of the bank with the hope that an agreement could be reached by negotiation. The bank officers refused to attend such a meeting. They insisted that applicants for positions were being chosen on their merits and that promotion policy also was based on merit. Further, they maintained that the coordinating committee of the civil rights organizations had no official standing or proper interest in the matter, which the management regarded as the bank's business.

As a result there was staged a "bank-in," which is still going on. Long lines of "customers" occupy the tellers with changing a dollar bill into 100 pennies and with changing 100 pennies into a dollar bill. At the same time crowds of demonstrators fill the bank lobby, chanting protest songs and shouting slogans à la college yells. All this is making it difficult for regular business to go on. Police officers summoned by the bank officials have asked the demonstrators to leave the premises. They have refused. Are they justified?

If the codes of moral theology and the proclaimed moral inhibitions of the Church are not absolute, certainly no more absolute are those of the State. In the end individual conscience has priority. "We must obey God rather than men" (Acts 5:29). But in trying to determine what is right in the given situation, one must evaluate the function of obedience to law. The publicity about the conflict, and what may be a sympathetic public response thereto, may be an aid in providing pressure on the legislators. Law and order serve the positive function of providing structures within which free decision-making is possible. Law and order enable one to live and plan with reliance on certain expectancies as to personal safety, continuity of the free use of property, the fulfillment of obligations, and so on. Hence, *supporting the law* by conforming to it is a positive contribution to one's fellows. In fact, it contributes to a person's own hopes for a more reliable fulfillment of his own chosen patterns of life.

However, where the law itself is demonic, that is, a structure of evil blocking opportunities for personhood to a serious degree, the breaking of the law may be the good. There still may be witness to the general value of structure by the acceptance with good grace of the penalties implied —with, of course, the use at the same time of every effort to procure either the legislative repeal or amendment of the given law or, through an appropriate legal case, a declaration of the unconstitutionality.[1]

Within these considerations, in CASE 70, *Red/green*, Myrtle's interesting, perhaps even sound, notions about color and traffic hardly provide a case for civil disobedience. The importance of support of general law-abiding,

[1] See more fully the author's *Doing the Truth*, rev. ed. (New York: The Macmillan Company, 1965), chap. 10, and Harrop A. Freeman, *et. al., Civil Disobedience* (Santa Barbara, Calif.: Center for the Study of Democratic Institutions, 1966).

the physical safety of herself and others, and the fulfillment of the legitimate expectancies of fellow motorists are of more significance than whatever value there may be in her acting out of an aesthetic theory.

The illegal operations of the physicians under the circumstances of CASE 73, *Secret nonconformity,* may very well have been ethically right on the theory that the specific and significant needs of human beings should take priority. While it is quite possible that the predominant motive, conscious or unconscious, of some of the physicians in some or all of their particular cases was profit, there is nothing that requires—or allows—this judgment as to motive.

Nevertheless, contrary to what the author (he is the bishop referred to in the Case) said publicly at the time, these actions are not in fact within the category of civil disobedience. Though with the required consent of the hospital's therapeutic abortion board, the operations were performed "in a corner," as it were. Not only was there no publicity, doubtless there was studious avoidance of it. Therefore these actions contributed nothing to the formation of public opinion or toward pressure for legislative reform—until, by investigation, they were discovered by law-enforcement officials. Though the balancing of claims was under a far better priority scale, the actions were no more civil disobedience than was bootlegging under the old Volstead Act. To say this is not to dispute the moral rightness of the acts, but simply to help us be clear about the meaning of civil disobedience.

For different reasons there is a basis for doubt as to whether the actions in CASE 74, *Civil disobedience/vigilantism,* fall in this category. Unlike CASE 70, *Red/green,* but like the Case just discussed above, at stake is a significant interest—here equal opportunity for hiring and promotion.

But this is precisely what the State Fair Employment Practices Law provides for and is designed to protect. Further, being violated are other good laws which the demonstrators are certainly not seeking to have repealed, namely, trespass, restraint of trade, unlawful assembly, and failure to obey an officer. In addition, inherent in the approach is a failure of due process. The civil rights coordinating committee has decided, rightly or wrongly, that the Fourth National Bank is in violation of the Fair Employment Practices Act, but the committee has not made use of the judicial process for which the Act provides. Thus a more apt tag than civil disobedience is "vigilantism."

When in the early days of San Francisco at the time of the gold rush an unofficial group of citizens, concerned about the widespread danger to life, limb, and property, decided that a fellow citizen had committed a crime and in a mob scene strung him up on a handy tree, in many cases the conclusion they drew may have been the right one; but in reaching the conclusion there was hardly a shred of due process. One of the traditions of the city is a certain romanticism about this aspect of the early days. The only reason this tradition is rather charming is the fact that there is virtually no chance of such a thing happening these days to anybody treasuring the tradition.

However, as in the case of the physicians, to say that the bank-in does not qualify as civil disobedience is not necessarily to say that it was unwarranted. It was argued by spokesmen for the coordinating committee that the F.E.P. Commission was understaffed (sufficient budget for it not having been provided by the legislature) and that the cumbersome procedures provided by the law resulted in delay which, as experience has shown, vitiated adequate relief. In support of this position they were able to point to the fact that, since the enactment of the law, only two cases processed had even reached the stage of enforcement through the courts and that in each of these cases the application had been thrown out by the judges. When the countering argument had been made that the route of legislative amendment should have been pursued first, the answer given was that this process would take a long time to determine what the civil rights advocates claimed already to know, namely, that there was little hope—particularly in a period of intense white backlash—that the Legislature would provide a more expeditious procedure and for more adequate staffing of the Commission.

A further argument was used: their methods get results. In support of this affirmation they pointed to three other operations in the previous year, sit-ins in a leading hotel, in a number of automobile dealers' establishments, and in a number of supermarkets, where in each case commitments were gained for equal opportunity in hiring and promotion. On the other hand, this latter argument is not without dubiety. That desired results had been achieved by an illegal action does not automatically validate the morality of the action. The same point could be made in defense of a thug who obtains a man's wallet by flashing a pistol. This Case illustrates that a moral decision must rest on a gestalt of factors which should be assessed and weighed in their connection with each other. The soundness or unsoundness of individual arguments taken separately does not determine the soundness or unsoundness of the decision reached.

For quite an opposite reason CASE 71, "*Live-in,*" possibly may not fall within the category of civil disobedience. There is a plausible point of constitutional law. It may be that under the umbrella of the Fourteenth Amendment a state—though it need not adopt a fair housing law—may not by purported repeal of such a law once adopted thus retrogress to what would in effect be state action denying what has been established as a right. Until the constitutional point is determined, the failure of the Andrewses to move at the expiration of their lease is superficially a violation of the civil law of contracts, and should they still not budge on the order of a sheriff, a violation of criminal strictures against trespass and refusal to obey an officer. But since the federal Constitution is paramount when any state or local law—either in general or as applied to particular categories of behavior—is in conflict with it, the "law" which the Andrewses would seem to be violating may actually be a *non-law*. Should that be the outcome, then there was no actual disobedience, civil or otherwise.

It should be noted that, contrary to popular impression, such organized or individual stubbornness is not simply a phenomenon of the political left. For the testing of constitutionality or legality, the normal way, exercised frequently ever since the beginning of the era of social legislation by firms of individuals and individuals, some of whom would fall within the political right, has been that of outright violation of what on the books are laws and regulations. This is illustrated by the action of the promoters in CASE 72, *Civil disobedience from the right.* Similarly, it is possible that the federal courts, in the injunction action which we can assume would be instituted by the S.E.C., might hold that the regulation in question was beyond the authority granted by Congress to the Commission. In this event it is a nonregulation; and thus the offering of the interests for sale is disobedience of nothing; it's just business as usual.

To return to the "live-in" device, let us make the assumption that the Fourteenth Amendment point would not be sustained by the courts, and that thus the discrimination is to be viewed not as State action but simply action of individuals and companies, against which the Constitution provides no protection and against which there is at present no state law. It could be argued that what under these circumstances is genuine civil disobedience has not been preceded by the "exhaustion of remedies" (to use, by analogy, the term for what is a sensible legal limitation requiring first appeal to any existing forms for relief). When a law is evil, or emasculated of its former good, normally a serious attempt at the procuring of adequate legislative action should come before organized disobedience. But it could be argued that the application of such a "condition precedent" in this situation would be fatuous. A good law had been passed and then deliberately repealed as a clear expression of the nonintegrationist views of a considerable majority of the populace. Delay in direct action in order to develop positive action toward a legislative—and, behind that, a popular—reversal would have little grounding in the likelihood of positive results. It may be that, in this grave pattern of injustice, the only hope lies in creating so widespread a pattern of nonconformity that either there just aren't enough sheriffs to handle the mass evictions and/or public or legislative opinion will be shocked into change at the sight of the attempt.

chapter 15

BEING RESPONSIBLE IN CONTEXT

Traditional systems of Code ethics, such as Thomistic moral theology, are divided into two main sections, general ethics and special ethics. The first part is devoted to general principles viewed as absolutes. The second part embodies subprinciples—also seen as absolutes—arranged according to various patterns of behavior.

No such division is possible under the heading "situation ethics." Situation ethics is "special ethics." Not special in the sense that there are abiding principles for the various categories of conduct. Special in the sense that situation ethics takes account of the particular situation, the uniqueness of each human relationship, the distinctiveness of each person.

Therefore, near the end of a casebook on situation ethics, the author need not be apologetic about his failure to cover all the areas of human life in encyclopedic fashion. A text with a Code approach to moral theology, on the other hand, would necessarily seek such comprehensiveness. Nevertheless, there are surely values to be found by developing illustrations in a number of fields. That is what this book has tried to do.

Illustrations drawn from a wide range of experience points up shortcomings in Code ethics (by showing that the supposed universality of such ethics is in fact limited). Second, reflection, with the aid of cases, on what persons (in contrast to things) are, can increase a person's awareness of his own positive intuitive response to goodness wherever and whenever he encounters it.

Such reflection can increase a person's awareness of the important factors that relate to any new situation. (And each situation is new!) At the same time, this process of weighing true-to-life data against a context equally true to life reveals the workings of ethical decision-making.

So we can say at this point that, while obviously not all situations have been covered, nearly all kinds of factors have been. Also, a method of deciding which factors to consider important has been demonstrated.

It now remains to turn again to our cases and seek to analyze the four Cases with which we began (pp. 1-5), both as a way of summarizing and also as a way of making more complete the discussion of sex—merely an area, not the entire terrain, of the "new morality."

Under Code morality, the problems posed are easy. In all four Cases, the answer is simply No.

Similarly, under the tenets of antinomianism, the Cases are simple. Since in such an outlook a recreational view of sex prevails, the answer in all four instances is Yes.

Under situation ethics, decision-making is not so easy. In fact, in the last analysis, no textbook answer can be given at all. No description of a real or a supposed situation can fully disclose the actual situation to which—with an approximation of reality—the description may point. *And there are no "pre-fab" answers apart from the particular facts outer and inner. There are no pre-fab answers in advance of the particular situation in the particular context.*

Nevertheless, such facts as are given in the four Cases suggest variants in the respective situations, variants that might make the difference between Yes and No. Among the factors that could be taken into account are these:

a. How valuable for the joy and fulfillment of the persons directly involved is the actual or proposed sexual intimacy?

b. How likely is the possibility of inequality? Is there imparity in the degree of caring, with one party becoming much more emotionally involved than the other, with the one not being ready (or perhaps able) to match the growing emotional involvement of the other?

c. How will their "going ahead" be likely to affect other obligations? How will ongoing commitments and the willingness and capacity to fulfill these commitments be affected?

Ask these questions about the situation in CASE 1, *We're all happier now*, and the prognosis of the relationships would seem to be favorable. A fuller, more happy life has, from all appearances, come to John and Mary. There seems to be sound and stable parity in their emotional involvement. Joan, the only other person in the picture, is apparently being denied nothing. In fact, there are even signs that there has been a gain where she is concerned.

Would this be true if she *knew?* Maybe not, but she doesn't know. Once a primary ethical decision has been made a particular way, more often than not secondary ethical responsibilities are entailed.

Here it may be that *discretion* would be among the second-level responsibilities, especially since in this situation there is no counterbalancing positive value for John, Mary, or others which could come from a more "open" situation.

But if reasonable care is the pattern, and high odds of success are apparent, the mere threat of a disrupting disclosure or some other harmful result is not an absolute determinant of a negative decision. If such mere threat of random danger were disabling, one wouldn't drive a car or take a plane!

When the same three questions are asked about CASE 2, *We're not hurting anybody,* it is easy to see that each of the answers would be somewhat more complex.

As to personal fulfillment, in CASE 1, the difference between No and Yes is a difference between o and +. In CASE 2, it is at most a difference between + and ++.

In fact, had Bill and Dorothy not been thrown together—more or less fortuitously it would seem—there might not have been the sudden contrast to the marital relationship each had back home. Perhaps conscious attention paid to the lost luster of the respective marriages could be enough to revitalize each, could shift each into a higher gear.

Should either Bill or Dorothy be capable of self-criticism and of taking a detached view, and if either or both were willing to act on such insight, it is quite possible that either of the marriages could be represented by a + large enough to equal or surpass the present ++. Such renewal of existing marital ties would have the additional result of ruling out the split-level view which generally is a minus factor in personal fulfillment and integration. In fact, the very existence of a Bill-Dorothy relationship can dull sensitivities to the need or possibilities of the renewal of the two marriages. It can, in fact, be a positive barrier to seeking or desiring such renewal.

There is also a strong possibility here of imparity—of inequality of involvement. Should one partner go deeper than the other in inner involvement, there is, at least at the present, an obvious block to a larger frame for such feelings, as the existence of reasonably sound marriages is presupposed (and a quick divorce and remarriage is consequently out of the question). Then where is the one left who has gotten in too deeply?

A measure of risk is also involved as far as the two marriages are concerned. Already we see that Bill and Dorothy (who share many interests) regard the occasions of their intimacy as more exciting than such encounters with their own spouses. Several other influences, clearly, are at work here: It is a *new* relationship. Human nature being what it is, the very fact of illicitness is exciting. So, too, the demands on imagination made by the need for secrecy. It all adds spice to the meetings. Hence, there is a competitive advantage to the outside liaison (one would say an unfair advantage, if that would not seem too judgmental).

Given these glamorizing elements, there are built-in distortions in the comparisons that Bill and Dorothy would naturally be making between their experiences and those at home. Hence, because sexual activity fuels a relationship at the same time as such activity expresses the relationship, growth in intensity seems likely. Bill and Dorothy may find themselves ensnared in a situation possibly destructive to the marriage of one, the other, or both. To the degree that their marriages are disabled, there will indeed be less willingness to fulfill the earlier commitments each has assumed as obligations.

Different again is the context created by CASE 3, *One-night stand.* As to the value of the joy and fulfillment achieved, it depends on the approach: whether one is focusing on the one night or on the life pattern for each.

From the first point of view, the value would seem to be relatively high; from the second, relatively low. In other words, gauging merely by standards of joy and fulfillment, or the possibility of imparity, no notable problem presents itself. Furthermore, it is presupposed that both Murray and Mildred are single and unentangled elsewhere. But before one would too hastily conclude with a Yes, at least some notice should be given to the fact that in the life pattern of each this encounter ranks fairly low. Still, then, there is a question as to whether this outcome, in this context, is appropriate.

The same question rises, but more sharply, when viewed all alone, as in CASE 4, *Services rendered.* In this situation the answers to the second and third of the questions (equality of involvement and previous commitment) are entirely simple.

There's no chance, to speak of, that either Joe or a Japanese prostitute will form an emotional involvement. Nor is their act likely to affect Joe's previous commitment, his marriage. There are thousands of miles between him and his home, and he has exercised prophylactic prudence.

Apart from other considerations, then, how much should be going between two persons for sexual intimacy to be appropriate? Intercourse is sometimes characterized as *sacramental.* A sacrament, in turn, is commonly defined as an outward and visible sign of an inward and spiritual grace.

If this characterization is appropriate, then we can go on and say that like other sacraments, the outward and visible aspect is both symbol of the inward and spiritual reality and also "means of grace." That is to say, it is a cause as well as an effect. It can strengthen and increase the inner tie.

Exponents of the recreational view of sex tend to allow for this dimension. Love, they say, makes things better. But still, they contend that love or no love, sex is better than no sex.

A meal—a great feast on a family or holiday occasion—can be charged with high significance. On the other hand, one sometimes is forced to "grab a bite," without the ceremony and the elevating atmosphere of a festive celebration. Usually, the argument-by-analogy goes, it is better to eat than not to eat.

The comparison is not entirely fair: Eating is essential to sustain life, while sex is not. Yet, as the analogy suggests, the act of sexual intercourse can serve as an end in itself or as that and also as the carrier of a personal relationship to one or another level of depth and commitment.

Not even Code ethicists today would want to deny that sex, whatever the requisites for its appropriate exercise, can be (and should be) recreation, indeed fun. The precise issues are these:

a. Is it right to be enjoying this fun without the existence of an inward and spiritual relationship?

b. If not, what degree of significance need the latter attain? And, more specifically, can this level of significance be attained outside marriage?

For light on the first question (Is recreation enough?) abstract reasoning is probably useless. In a text on ethics written eleven years ago the author resorted to the following logic:

Sexual intercourse is sacramental in nature; ergo, it is sacrilegious when there is not the requisite inward and spiritual union, namely, marriage.[1] However sound or un-

[1] *Doing the Truth* (New York: Doubleday & Company, 1955), pp. 128–29; but cf. the revised edition (New York: The Macmillan Company, 1965), pp. 154–158.

sound may be the norm thus derived (no marriage, no sex), and we will presently come to this question, the point is not established by reasoning. There are two difficulties: Even granted that sex can only be viewed as sacramental, this does not necessarily require the conclusion that the only qualifying inward and spiritual union would be one legalized by marriage. Further, simply to affirm that sex by its very nature is sacramental is to beg the question which the existence of the recreational view raises: the conclusion is embraced within the premise chosen.

For the consistent situation ethicist, the only light available is that which may come from the data of experience, personal or vicarious, and its projection focused toward a given situational context, as to likely reactions or effects. The following would be among the considerations:

a. Does a pattern of casualness tend to blunt sex as an instrument for expressing "the real thing"? Or, does frequent sex with a variety of partners extend one's sexual responsiveness, spontaneity of effective technique, and aliveness to "sexual signals" with a favorable effect on its use as an instrument for expressing love with commitment?

b. In our culture, casual sex more often than not calls for secrecy and a certain amount of scheming. Does a pattern of such arrangements, of increasingly sophisticated deceit, tend to develop a habit of deceit in other areas of life? Can it be assumed that persons cannot "specialize" in their deception—being open in other respects? As the C.I.A. agent's tenure lengthens, does he become less straightforward in all other aspects of his life?

c. Speaking of furtiveness, is it not likely that the spice which its exercise adds to the mix, enhancing the salaciousness of the occasions, can exaggerate the real importance of the meetings?

d. The experience of many counselors shows that most couples who have been to bed together, if they continue to see each other, are likely, in spite of interim resolutions, to continue the pattern. That being the case, what if there is not much in such a relationship? Can it have deteriorated into a mere "servicing" one of the other? Maybe both really would rather end the evening early and get to bed—individually—to sleep. If this is the way it is, or has become, how much harm is likely to result if either or both drift out of the relationship? Or, if the parties are going to be seeing each other from time to time anyway, if it would seem that on a later meeting, one or both would probably be getting something out of a return to the earlier pattern, won't the result be good? In any event, who is harmed?

e. In order to isolate a precise point for consideration in the statement of the possible factors, pro and con, we have excluded the matter of commitments to others whether these are marital partners or not. For this next pair of possible factors we should assume that one or both of the parties has a really significant ongoing relationship. Also, we should assume that there is no likelihood of the loved one's finding out. And lastly, we assume that there is almost no chance that this indulgence in casual sex will set off a deeper involvement on either side. Yet is it not possible or likely that the very fact of casual sex may unconsciously effect a change in one or both of the persons—a change which may be detected by the partner back home? This, then, may well cause a breakdown in vital communication ties, because of the growth of a "silent sector," an exception to the complete openness that had prevailed.

f. To bring in guilt, as such, at this point would obviously beg the question. But no one could deny that a *sense* of guilt is a fact, and furthermore that such a sense of guilt is fairly widespread among persons who have engaged in casual sex. So, recognizing this as part of the data, is it good to do something that will leave one or both parties burdened in this way? Of course, if one does not credit such guilt feelings, he might counter by asking, Would I not be contributing to the development of personal freedom in myself and in my companion by mutually reasoning it out and acting out our arrived-at conclusions?

For those readers whose estimate of their answers to the above questions leads them to the conclusion that there need be no additional justification for sex other than the opportunity and the desire for recreation, then consideration of the second question (How significant need the inward relation be?) is superfluous. For these people if it happens in a given connection that there is a level of inward involvement, fine. Indeed, perhaps the more the better.

For those who come out the other way, however, who conclude from an analysis like the above that an inward reality is vital for appropriate outward sexual expression, an important question remains: *How much?*

An easy answer is simply, marriage. This reply matches that of the Code ethicists, who specialize in pat answers. But for the situation ethicist, several difficulties with the answer would have to be taken into account.

First, the mere possession of a marriage license does not guarantee a significant inward and spiritual relationship. Married couples who rarely engage in sex or who are legally separated or who are living daily with a wall of hostility and yet engage in a "servicing" kind of relationship all attest to the difficulties facing the Code ethicist at this point. Let him give "marriage" as his answer, and he still must face the implications of situations such as those portrayed above. Here is a real ethical question under his sacramental view of sex. This question also can vex the situation ethicist who expects some significant personal meaning to prevail in the sexual act.

Again, for the antinomist, no problem: for him, recreation is all (and marriage or lack of it is of scant concern).

On the other hand, widespread experience verifies the fact that there are frequent personal ties, mental and emotional, between unmarried persons. The most obvious evidence of this recurring phenomenon is that for this very reason (or sometimes because of an illusion that it is true) lots of couples get married! But equally obvious is the fact that such a reality does not automatically disappear when for one reason or another marriage does not occur; there is no statute of limitations that at a certain point brings an end to such reality.

Marriage or no, spiritual relationship can be at various levels. There is the old-fashioned distinction between like, love, and in love. Or in somewhat more recent categories, meeting, rapport, recognition, commitment (and the latter in varying degrees). Except for the most inhibited persons, there is spontaneously some measure of physical expression for any of these levels of relationships with persons of the opposite sex.

Counselors, parental or otherwise, trained or amateur, inevitably tend to be rather imprecise in answering the common question of youth: "How far can I go?" Add to this problem an additional consideration (one that would be particularly significant in situation ethics) of the unique character of each of the parties involved, the unique character of the particular relationship, and the unique character of the whole context at the given time the question is being asked. It becomes obvious that there is no way to build a standard set of answers for the young—or for anyone.[2]

What's the value of raising the question then? Because if it is reasonably assumed, as we have in this part of the chapter, that there should be a correlation between interpersonal meaning and sexual action, this question is *the* question. It is fundamental, or at least prior, to what may be other important questions already considered (the dynamics of parity/imparity; likely effects of other commitments and effects on others).

The fact that a tidy group of prefab answers cannot be supplied does not minimize its significance. In fact, even a well-meaning attempt at this point in the book to supply them would disappoint even the most casual reader. It would be quite inconsistent with the entire methodology of the approach to ethics espoused, with, hopefully, some plausibility.

Thus we see illustrated in our consideration of decision-making in the area of sex what is true across the board. To these things, Yes:

A responsible approach to all decisions.
The rating of persons above things.
The valuing of *erōs* love ahead of all other responses.
Fulfillment and service as the style of life.
Serious attention to the relevant portions of the Code as representing generalizations of human experience with common problems.
Awareness of pertinent factors to be weighed on the scales.

[2] *Loc. cit.;* see also the author's *Teenagers and Sex* (Englewood Cliffs, N.J.: Prentice-Hall, 1965), pp. 79–81.

No, then, to *ready-made* answers for particular decisions required of people.

A greater awareness of these Yes's and this No, and greater maturity in the application of them to the marvelous diversity in the flow of life, has been the purpose of the pages of this casebook.

INDEX

Entries in boldface type indicate the principal discussion of the topic.

SCRIPTURAL REFERENCES

OLD TESTAMENT

NEW TESTAMENT